THE KITCHEN
PLANNER

THE KITCHEN PLANNER

ROBIN MURRELL

MITCHELL BEAZLEY

THE KITCHEN PLANNER
Robin Murrell

Edited and designed by Mitchell Beazley
International Ltd, Michelin House, 81 Fulham Road,
London SW3 6RB

Managing Editor Frank Wallis

Editors Leonie Hamilton and Alan Folly
Picture Research Anne-Marie Ehrlich
Illustrations Anthony Curtiss and David Ashby
Cover photograph James Merrell
Production Philip Collyer

Previously published as **Small Kitchens**
© Mitchell Beazley International Ltd 1986
Text © Robin Murrell 1986
Artwork © Mitchell Beazley International Ltd 1986
First paperback edition 1993

ISBN 185732 094 8

The publishers have made every effort to ensure that
all instructions given in this book are accurate and
safe, but they cannot accept liability for any resulting
injury, damage or loss to either person or property
whether direct or consequential and howsoever
arising. The author and publishers will be grateful for
any information which will assist them in keeping
future editions up to date.

Typeset by Servis Filmsetting Ltd, Manchester
Reproduction by Anglia Reproductions Ltd, Witham,
Essex
Produced by Mandarin Offset
Printed and bound in Hong Kong
D.L. NA.283-1986

CONTENTS

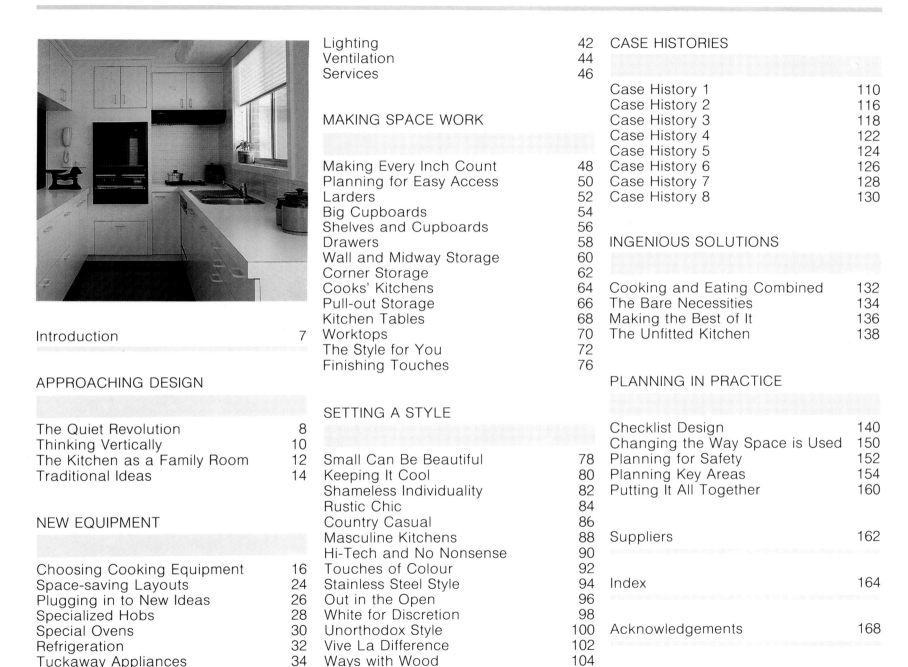

INTRODUCTION

Kitchens, like most things, are subject to fashion and to change in social attitudes and aspirations. The well-to-do Victorian housewife had a large kitchen, but one in which she seldom if ever worked: her role was to approve the menus and to check the accounts while hired staff did the work. Today those who use kitchens not only expect to do the work themselves, they expect it to be physically easy – if creatively challenging; they expect the setting in which they do it to be stylish, and they expect the rest of the family to be actively involved.

But today's needs do not always match the allocation of space in yesterday's buildings. Many people have to live in houses or apartments designed for an earlier generation. Somehow, the kitchen has to be altered or adapted so that advantage can be taken of the savings, both in labour and time, offered by advanced technology, so that more than one person can use it at the same time, and so that it looks good. Frequently the fundamental problem is one of space. Not only are most new houses smaller than those of the past, more and more people are moving into city apartments where space, often converted from some other use, is limited. At the same time, storage needs in kitchens have become greater as people acquire a greater range of modern labour-saving appliances and stock a wider range of cooking ingredients.

In time, kitchens will probably become larger again in response to the new perception of their role in the home, but this process will take many years. In the meantime, if the kitchen you have is too small, you have three options: you can move somewhere else with more kitchen space; you can try to make more space available where you are; or you can try to make better use of the space you have – the problem with which this book is primarily concerned.

The leading makers of kitchen furniture and equipment have responded to this problem with a host of new ideas on how to use space more effectively and with some exciting new ideas on the design of cooking and other appliances. These new developments and how they influence the planning of the working areas and the room's decoration are all examined in detail in *The Kitchen Planner*.

Some of the design recommendations that emerge may be unexpected. For instance, there are practical limits to how small in size hobs and ovens can be made because they still have to be able to accommodate pans of normal size. So instead, makers have invented ways to make better use of the space such items occupy and have made the items themselves far more versatile. You might not think that in the context of a small kitchen a big sink or a ventilated larder for food storage would be recommended, yet both of these items have an essential role in the latest thinking about efficient use of working and cupboard space.

The Kitchen Planner is less concerned however, with theories about ergonomics or domestic interior architecture than it is with setting out down-to-earth ideas about how you can improve your own kitchen. Whether you are simply updating part of your furnishings or equipment, or undertaking a complete refurbishment, you should find all the information here that you need to guide you through the maze of alternative ways of tackling the job.

THE QUIET REVOLUTION

Most people have kitchens which are smaller than they would like and many have kitchens which, because of poor planning, feel smaller than they really are. All small kitchens start off with one natural virtue – nothing needed can be very far away. However, the smaller the kitchen the easier it is to fritter away this potential advantage by making things used regularly more difficult to get at than is necessary or by creating working areas that are completely inadequate.

The very best kitchen designs are those in which all tasks can be carried out with a minimum of labour and fatigue. To achieve this ideal you have to choose the right equipment, plan the working areas and related storage to achieve the best compromise possible in the space available, and finally create an "atmosphere" that is right for you and other regular users of the room.

The four basic rules that are the key to success in designing small kitchens are these:

1 The more frequently any item is used, the more readily accessible it should be;

2 Make your working areas as adaptable as possible, so that you get the maximum use out of available space;

3 Save space on equipment and invest it in workspace and storage;

4 Make sure your kitchen is "friendly" – use as much care in planning colour, safety, lighting and ventilation as you do in choosing your cooker.

The mistake which many people make when planning a new kitchen is first to find a range of furniture they like and then to see how many cupboards they can fit into the space available. They postpone worrying about where individual items of equipment, utensils and cookwares, dried and fresh food and so on will be stored until after the kitchen has been installed. That approach never works satisfactorily.

Another common mistake is to rely entirely on someone else to design your kitchen for you. The spaces available vary in shape and character and the needs of every family are to some extent unique. It is thus essential that everyone who uses the kitchen contributes to the design.

The return of the kitchen to its earlier role as a family room as well as a household workshop is part of a quiet revolution which has been taking place in domestic design over the past ten years or so. Another aspect of that revolution is the development that has taken place in kitchen equipment. Manufacturers are now making it easier than ever before to pack essential cooking and other appliances into incredibly small spaces. This means that if you are planning the refurbishment of a small kitchen you do not have to start off with a host of full-sized machines and then try to jam the working areas and storage into the space that is left. New types of sinks, cookers, food preparation machines and laundering equipment that are now available take up less space, work faster and use much less energy than their equivalents of a decade or so ago.

At the same time, leading furniture designers have started to rethink accepted ideas on the use of space in kitchens. For instance, the "working triangle" approach to design, which evolved in the days when it was rare for more than one person to use the kitchen at a time, does not work in a family kitchen where two or three people may be doing potentially conflicting jobs at the same time. As a result, we are now seeing less "science" and more common sense being applied to planning kitchens and their furnishings.

Oddly enough, designers have looked back a century or more for ideas on how to make today's kitchens pleasanter and more efficient to work in. So we now find that some of the best designs contain modern versions of the dresser, the larder, the kitchen table and even yesterday's giant china sinks.

Finally there is style. Today most people agree that it is as important to create a friendly, inviting visual atmosphere in the kitchen as it is in any other room in the house. However, many people also make the mistake of confusing style with design and the result can be disastrous, especially in a small kitchen.

Design in the context of the kitchen means getting the layout right, selecting the correct equipment and planning the storage of utensils, cookwares, china, foods and other ingredients plus all the further impedimenta of the modern kitchen. Only then should you start thinking about details of style, such as colour schemes, tiling or furniture finishes.

The essence of today's best kitchens – style, flair, yet total practicality. In this Allmilmö kitchen the space is compact and everything in regular use is immediately to hand. The design is visually stimulating but function has not been neglected in the creation of an exciting form. Practicality also lies behind the choice of materials. Note the virtual absence of plastics and the use of wood furniture in a way that would be complementary to an adjoining dining area; the virtually indestructible but pretty ceramic sink; and the tiled working surfaces which are proof against heat and cutting damage. The tall cabinets with semi-opaque doors to left and right revive traditional dresser storage thinking and the angled doors cleverly create more sense of space. The compact multi-function oven and ceramic hob offer gourmet cooking facilities linked to unobtrusive styling. At night the concealed lighting above and below the cabinets will subtly present the geometry of this kitchen in a quite different way without leaving any blind spots in the working areas.

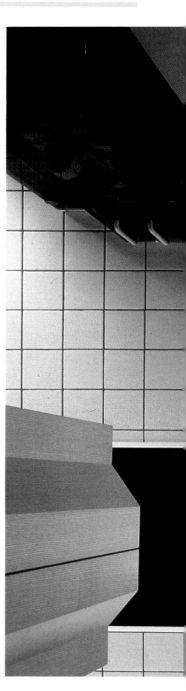

THINKING VERTICALLY

The smaller the kitchen, the easier it is to lose things in it – because when space is at a premium we tend to pack things onto shelves in cupboards without much thought for how easy they will be to find later. The same goes for worktops, which get cluttered with gadgets, utensils, storage jars and plug-in electrical equipment so you find that you have to move things just to find space to work on.

All real kitchens contain a certain amount of amiable clutter, but it is all too easy to have too much of a good thing. However, it is rarely the fault of the user if things get out of hand. The blame lies with the person who designed the kitchen because

he or she failed to remember one of the most important rules of good kitchen planning – if it is difficult to get at things, it will be twice as difficult to put them away.

In a badly-designed kitchen the items which you use most often get left where they stand. This may not matter so much in a large kitchen because you can move from one work area to another according to what you happen to be doing, but in a small kitchen you probably won't have that option. The chances are that you only have one decent working area anyway, which must be easy to keep reasonably clear so that it is ready for the next job.

This is not as difficult to achieve as it sounds, because you use only the front half of a working surface for actively working on anyway. The back half is used to store temporarily the things you are using at that moment – the food mixer or processor if you are making pastry or shredding or slicing vegetables; containers of ingredients, herbs or spices; food which you are in the course of preparing or which has been prepared in advance.

Therefore the trick in the case of a small kitchen is to store everything you use regularly where it can be reached with a minimum of effort.

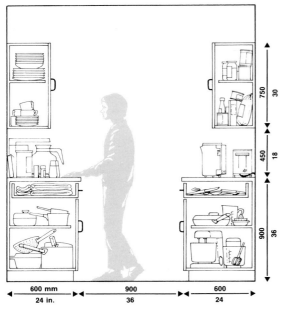

WRONG: *Most of us are all too familiar with the kitchen situation above. Trying to obtain the maximum amount of worktop length actually achieves the least usable space, because worktops get cluttered with the items you use most and to which you need quick access. Fixed shelves in cupboards mean stacking the contents if space is not to be wasted, making access difficult.*

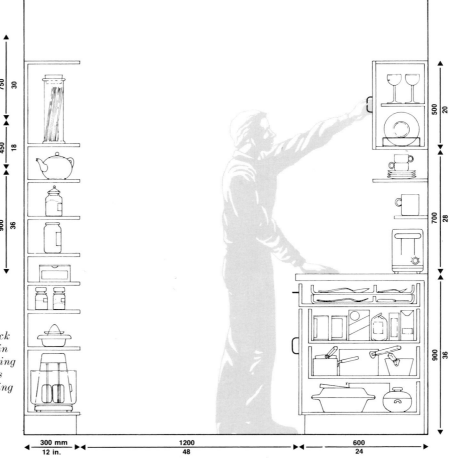

CORRECT: *Big changes are: worktops concentrated in planned "work zone" arrangements; storage planned for maximum access, with most-used items readily to hand on "midway" shelves and racks; tall, shallow storage cupboards with lots of adjustable shelves set as close as possible for minimum waste of space and contents kept one item deep whenever possible. Two-layer divided trays in drawers for cutlery and pull-out shelves below mean everything comes easily to hand. Even the plinth space is used for spare tins, bulbs or kitchen tools.*

Look round your present kitchen and check how many items which you use more or less every day are either out of sight or hidden behind something else. If the answer is "very few" the chances are that you quite like your kitchen as it is and enjoy working in it. However, if the answer is "many of the items I use regularly are difficult to get at (if they are put away in their proper places)" you probably don't enjoy working in that kitchen much and spend an excessive amount of time tidying up.

The two diagrams here illustrate the right and wrong ways to plan storage around your main working area. Note how, without using any more actual space, far more accessible storage capacity has been created in the second example and that the "movement space" between cupboards is actually greater.

The key point is that in the second example the use of space has been planned from the floor up, using every inch available and ensuring that everything in daily use can be reached without bending, stretching or reaching over other items. Note that this has been achieved without using any costly specialized fittings.

In any kitchen the most important area of storage space is between hip-height and shoulder-height. Anything stored in this zone can be reached without bending or stretching and nothing which is in regular use should be kept at a higher or lower level than this area of "maximum access". The smaller the kitchen the more important it is to make use of every inch of wall space within this zone.

Note that at lower levels pull-out storage shelves make good use of space which would otherwise be very difficult to reach (even if you can remember what is stored there). And the "plinth" zone just above floor level, easier and safer to reach than the space above a wall cupboard, is the ideal place to store tools or rarely-used items.

Every item stored in this central kitchen working area is easy to find, easy to reach and therefore easy to put away again. There are a variety of different types of storage to suit the entire range of utensils, kitchenwares, ingredients, pans and other items you would want to store this close to hand. Storage systems as flexible and well-designed as this are now available in virtually any kind of furniture style you care to name.

THE KITCHEN AS A FAMILY ROOM

Whatever shape or size your family happens to be, the chances are that all its members will, at some time, end up in the kitchen. However small today's kitchens are, they therefore have to be designed for use by several people at the same time.

When working out your personal pattern of kitchen living, don't just think of the family as that statistical parents-plus-2.4-children unit. The chances are that your basic family makeup is not like this and in any case allowance has to be made for your wider "family" – other relatives, friends and casual acquaintances who from time to time take up space in your kitchen, whether or not they are actually doing anything constructive or useful while they are there.

There are two common causes of conflict for space. People may simply be visiting, without actually getting involved in cooking, washing up or any other work. Or one person may be trying to prepare a major meal while another is putting together a quick snack.

The answer in both instances is to think of the kitchen as containing two distinct areas – the inner kitchen where the main food preparation, cooking and probably dishwashing go on and a secondary area where people can make coffee or a snack without interfering or getting in the way. When you think of the kitchen in terms of primary and secondary work zones in this way simple common sense is sufficient to enable you to decide where the essential equipment should be placed.

The illustration on these pages shows that a fixed table forms the division between the primary and secondary areas in the kitchen. The heart of the primary area is the brilliant multi-purpose Pallas system sink (Villeroy & Bóch). A fully-integrated dishwasher is set to the left and a ceramic hob has been fitted flush in the table surface, so that it doubles as a working or eating area when cool. The controls are in the rack above, out of harm's way. The person working at the sink only has to make a half-turn to reach the cooking area and, though there is a plate's width between the back of the hob and the other side of the centre table, it is quite practical to serve from pans on the further side of the hob or even to cook from both sides.

The fridge, freezer, main oven/grill and secondary oven/microwave have all been placed in the secondary area. According to the old "working triangle" theory this is wrong, but in a kitchen as small as this it means that valuable storage space

is available, in the primary area, for often-used utensils, chinaware and supplies.

There is plenty of space to pass behind someone sitting at the end of the table to reach the secondary working area, which is also a complete working zone in itself. Anyone wanting to make coffee or a snack in this kitchen can get at virtually everything they need (apart from water) without going into the primary working area. The trick is to place the fridge and the main foodstore in positions that make them equally accessible from both the primary and secondary areas. Although in this case due to shortage of space the larder had to be sited just outside the kitchen itself in a lobby through an archway, it is still within easy reach from either side of the kitchen.

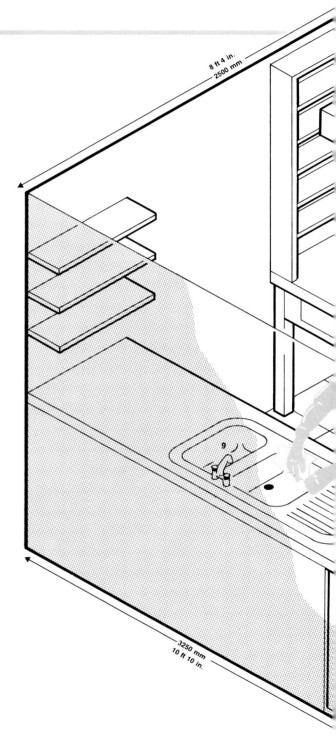

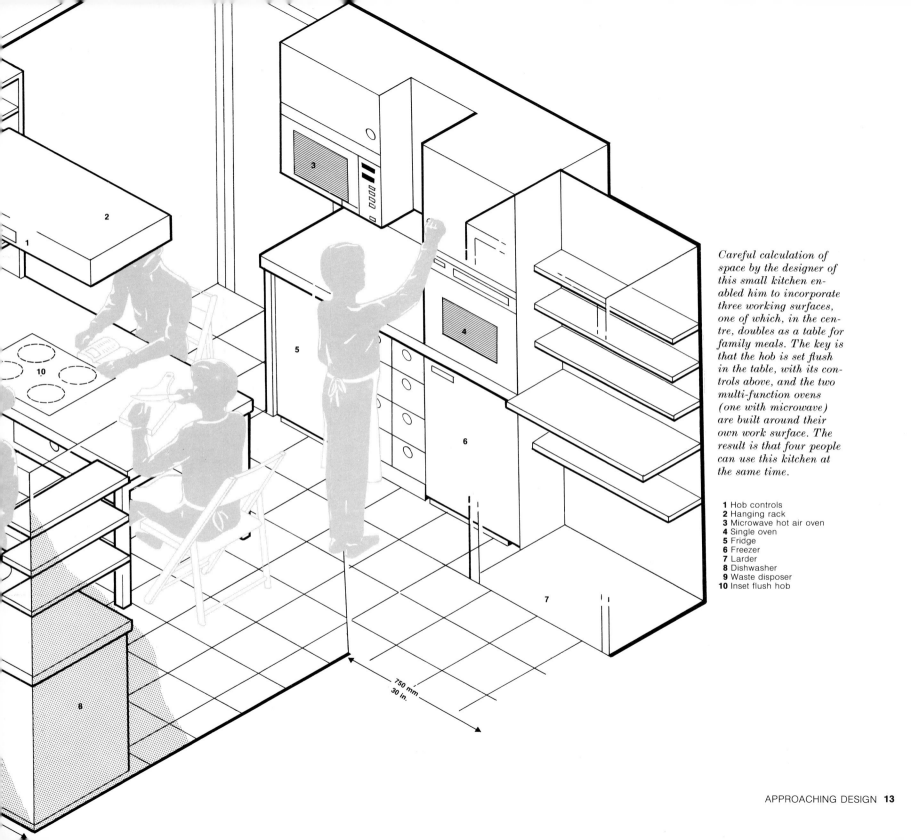

Careful calculation of space by the designer of this small kitchen enabled him to incorporate three working surfaces, one of which, in the centre, doubles as a table for family meals. The key is that the hob is set flush in the table, with its controls above, and the two multi-function ovens (one with microwave) are built around their own work surface. The result is that four people can use this kitchen at the same time.

1 Hob controls
2 Hanging rack
3 Microwave hot air oven
4 Single oven
5 Fridge
6 Freezer
7 Larder
8 Dishwasher
9 Waste disposer
10 Inset flush hob

750 mm
30 in.

TRADITIONAL IDEAS

The idea of looking back to the 19th-century heyday of classic, heavily-staffed "backstairs" kitchens for ways of solving problems that arise in planning today's much smaller kitchens may sound odd. Yet people had to work so hard in those kitchens that they had to be laid out and furnished functionally. As no-one gave a second thought to style in what were considered to be little more than utilitarian "food factories", trends in fashion or furniture design were not allowed to override practical considerations.

Kitchens of the 19th century had certain design features in common – open-shelf storage for those items most often in use; a large walk-in larder or ventilated foodstore; a central working table which could be used by several people at the same time; and at least one very large sink. What we are now discovering is that, even in the smallest kitchen, modern versions of these items are the key to making the best use of limited space.

Open shelves provide more accessible storage and take up less space than any form of cupboard. If the kitchen is properly ventilated (and unfortunately very few small kitchens are), dirt is simply not the problem everyone expects it to be; and, in any case, if the items concerned are in constant use they get washed regularly.

Don't let bad ventilation (and the dirty, germ-ridden surfaces which result) be an excuse for hiding everything away in cupboards. Solve the ventilation problem (see pages 44–45) and keep those items that are in constant use ready to hand at all times. Unnecessary cupboard doors in a small kitchen are a waste of space, dangerous, irritating and simply make things much less accessible.

However, it is not necessary that everything should be stored in the open. Confine dresser storage and hanging racks to those utensils, foods, ingredients and other items that are in use at least once every day. Note that these are also the items that need to be stored in the primary working area in the kitchen.

A properly-planned larder or ventilated foodstore enables you to pack more items into less space than any other form of cupboard. The best modern larders have racks on the back of the door (or doors) for small jars and such things as ketchup bottles plus lots of shelves of different depths and at different spacings so that no item ever needs to be hidden behind another. Such foodstores should always have through ventilation,

which can usefully form part of the total ventilation system of the kitchen.

It may seem paradoxical to recommend the fitting of a large cupboard in a small space, but in a larder you can concentrate more enclosed storage into a smaller floor area than by any other means. Also, remember that most items in a larder are within that magical "maximum access" zone between hip and shoulder height.

The equivalent of the traditional table makes an excellent focal point for non-working visitors, breakfasting and light family meals, hobbies, homework and all the dozens of other activities that make up the role of the kitchen as a family room. It is the ideal height for cooking and heavy food preparation (chopping and pastry-making by hand, for example). Such a surface forms a natural division between the primary and secondary areas and in many other ways becomes perhaps the most important element in a total design. As you will see later, it is therefore worth going to considerable lengths to find ways to fit a table, peninsula or bar into even the most awkward space.

The vogue for tiny round kitchen sinks which swept the market in the late 1970s had much more to do with fashion than practicality. It was often suggested that they were the ideal shape for dishwashing but no-one ever explained what you were supposed to do with large roasting-tins or oven shelves.

The latest multi-purpose "system sinks" have taken much of the drudgery, backache and unpleasantness out of wet food preparation and the cleansing of utensils, pans or china that cannot await the next dishwasher load. Different makers offer many alternatives in materials, shapes and sizes, and specialized fittings. The best answer is to get your hands on working examples of as many alternatives as possible to see which system will work best for you.

In the context of a modern kitchen the term "pull out baskets" has come to mean chromed or plastic-covered wirework. Yet there is much to be said for using traditional materials such as wicker for storing vegetables. These vegetable baskets can be taken right out and carried to the working surface so that you can pre-sort fresh foods before starting to prepare a meal. Some would argue that they are also "friendlier" than those made of modern materials.

A modern example of a traditional idea, in which dresser-style cupboards have been set above a marble pastry-making surface. Efficient use has been made of the space, with instant access to everything required. Still the best material on which to make pastry and carry out other food-mixing tasks, the stone surface is attractive as well as practical and durable. Woodstock specialize in reinterpreting traditional kitchen features like these without attempting self-conscious reproductions of old furniture.

CHOOSING COOKING EQUIPMENT 1

WHAT DO YOU COOK AND HOW DO YOU COOK IT?

The range of cooking equipment now available is quite bewildering. It is all too easy to be distracted by the razzmatazz surrounding all the new ideas which are flooding onto the market and to end up buying equipment that simply does not fit in with the way you approach cooking.

One reaction might be to play it safe and go for a cooker with which you are familiar. That would be a great pity because what might now be called conventional cooking equipment tends to be bulkier, slower and a good deal more expensive to run than the best of the new hobs and ovens that are becoming readily available.

However, you are certainly right to be cautious. There is nothing more infuriating than spending a great deal of money on an exciting new item of cooking equipment only to discover that it will not produce the results you are expecting. This has been more of a problem since it became commonplace for ovens and hobs to cross national borders as there is a great difference in the way in which people use cookers and their accessories in different countries.

For instance, throughout Europe experts have been arguing for years now on what "brown" means. The reason is that, in defining standard tests for cooking performance, you have to agree what things should look like when they have been cooked. But it appears that "brown" means different things to cooks in Munich, Milan, Marseilles and Manchester. To make matters worse, in Britain baking performance is traditionally tested with batches of fairy cakes whereas on the Continent they do it by cooking sablé biscuits. The only answer is to insist on a live demonstration of any cooking equipment with which you are not already familiar, and ensure that it involves methods of cooking which are important to you and recipes you use often.

Grilling, high-temperature roasting and slow simmering are the three cooking methods which you are most likely to want to check out because they best reveal the differences between cookers. Also, if you use specialized cookwares such as terracotta pots or a wok, make certain that the type of hob you are considering will be suitable.

Incidentally, you may have noticed an emphasis on hobs and ovens rather than on complete one-piece cookers. The reason is that there is no longer any justification, even on cost

grounds, for installing one-piece floor-standing cookers in small kitchens. In limited space it is even more dangerous and inconvenient to use a low-level oven than it is in a larger room.

It used to be argued that split-level cooking arrangements take up more space than one-piece cookers, but now that we have a new generation of very compact ovens that is no longer so. The advantages of separating the hob (which should be in the primary working area) from the oven (which may well be better placed in the secondary area) and of fitting each of them at the most convenient heights for the users involved are so great that they should be sacrificed only in special circumstances and after very careful thought.

How many cook in your kitchen?

The more people who want to cook at the same time, the more difficult it is to work out an arrangement that will avoid clashes. If the kitchen happens to be small as well, it makes the problem that much more interesting.

Let us take a typical "worst case" situation. Imagine that two people are sharing the preparation of a normal evening meal while two others are trying to get themselves quickly-cooked snacks. If the snack-makers are normal teenagers, they will probably want quite different items, but at the same time.

If all you have to cook on is an orthodox, floor-standing one-piece cooker, someone is going to have to give way. If you also have a microwave cooker, that, depending on what you wish to cook, may make the situation a little easier, but not much.

However, imagine for a moment that the hob and main oven are quite separate and that the hob is placed in such a way that it can be used by two or more people at the same time. Then add a microwave oven which can also bake or grill. Suddenly the problems fade away.

There are many other ways in which one can exploit the versatility of today's cooking equipment to solve similar problems of space and numbers. Where ovens are concerned, the much greater versatility of the latest equipment overcomes many difficulties. Multi-function ovens are discussed in greater detail on the next page, but if you are either buying or replacing a microwave cooker it is well worth considering one of the more sophisticated machines that also roasts and bakes.

The fact that a kitchen is small and perhaps also an unusual shape need not be a reason to compromise in your choice of cooking equipment. This kitchen has been laid out to suit its position at one end of a room which also includes dining and sitting areas, yet more than adequate space has been created to accommodate a four-burner gas hob and a large sink. In other words, the equipment has been selected to do the job required and the layout planned around it. Note the clever, strongly-built pull-out shelf on which the food mixer sits permanently, with accessories readily to hand in the area beneath.

Ovens

There are now a large number of ovens on the market that offer combinations of cooking systems. Not only does this "multi-function" feature considerably increase the usefulness of the equipment concerned, it also solves to some extent the problem of having to choose between one system and another when you may not have adequate experience of the alternatives.

Several of the most interesting models available are described on the following pages, but it may be helpful to explain the meaning of some of the cooking system names now commonly used by makers.

Radiant oven

The conventional electric oven system in which the space is heated by fixed elements controlled by a thermostat. These elements may be hidden behind removable panels in the side of the oven or, in some Continental designs, below a plate in the base. Most ovens of this type are available with "stay clean" linings, but it must be remembered that these work well only at high temperatures and most have a limited effective life.

The main disadvantage of radiant electric ovens is that they have to be pre-heated, which may take quite a long time. For this and other reasons they are not very efficient. Also, because the oven interior casing tends to be hotter than the food being cooked, food residues tend to bake on and regular cleaning is essential.

Fan-assisted oven

Basically this is quite similar to a radiant electric oven, but a circulating fan is used to even out the temperature variations between one part of the oven and another and also to shorten pre-heating times.

Hot-air oven

A totally different electric cooking system that relies on the high-speed circulation of air heated by a hidden element in the back (or sometimes in the side) of the oven compartment. Pre-heating time is virtually eliminated and cooking temperatures (which tend to be the same throughout the whole oven space) can generally be reduced by somewhere between 10 per cent and 20 per cent. Such ovens are therefore much more efficient and convenient to use. However, it is worth checking the top temperature at which a model will cook because some of the less expensive hot-air ovens do not roast particularly well.

Hot-air ovens have two other important advantages. They are inherently clean, because the interior casing rarely gets hot enough for food residues to burn on and, because the air flow is continually being passed over the heating element, and foods being cooked tend to seal completely, flavours do not transfer from one dish to another. You will therefore find that you can cook a fish dish, roast pork and bake an apple flan in the same oven at the same time without one tasting of the other. Thorough cleaning tends to be necessary only three or four times a year.

If you have not used a really good quality hot-air oven before, there is a pleasant surprise in store for you. For instance, if you need a quick Victoria sandwich, you can put the two tins of sponge mix into a stone cold oven, switch on and receive a perfect cake 15 minutes later.

Microwave

Please do not call a conventional microwave cooker an oven, because it isn't. The only thing a microwave cooker can do is heat water (or ice, if the water happens to be frozen) – but, as most foods contain water, it is a versatile alternative to orthodox boiling or casseroling.

Microwave cookers are ideal for defrosting and for reheating. They cook fish and most vegetables quite beautifully and, with a little skill and practice, can also be used for a wide variety of other foods. They also work cleanly and efficiently.

However, there is no escaping the fact that the appearance of many foods cooked in a microwave is not the same as it would be in a conventional oven. It is for this reason that the usefulness of a microwave is considerably increased if you choose a model that also has a radiant or hot-air cooking facility. You then have the best of both worlds because, to take one example, with this type of cooker you can roast a chicken in half the time and at a quarter of the cost of doing the same job in any other sort of oven yet it will look and taste as if it had been cooked conventionally. And don't forget

that such "microwave-combination" cookers tend to be far smaller, not to mention cheaper, than ordinary built-in ovens.

For some people, one of the larger microwave-combination cookers may be the only oven needed, because they are quite capable of handling the whole roasting and baking requirements of two people or perhaps even more. However, most people will use them as an alternative to a second conventional oven in a kitchen with large and varied cooking requirements, if only because they are really handy for warming plates – something of which a straightforward microwave cooker is quite incapable.

Multi-function ovens

Appliances which offer you the option, at the turn of a dial or by touch-control programming, of several different cooking systems singly or in combination. Typical of the combined cooking systems offered by such ovens are microwave and hot-air; microwave and radiant browning; overhead grill and intermittent air circulation; and programmed pre-roasting followed by microwave-only finishing.

Grills and browners

Most multi-function ovens contain grilling elements, though in many cases their maximum power is not great enough to approach the performance of a good gas grill. If you mainly use a grill for browning, as distinct from searing meat, a multi-function oven will probably be adequate, but if not, you should test the oven you have in mind before buying it to ensure it will meet your requirements.

A technique that is unique to the best hot-air ovens is thermo-grilling. Chops, sausages, steaks or fish can be set out on an open wire shelf and then cooked in the hot air flow with the temperature at the maximum setting. The effect is not unlike a rotisserie, except that the air turns round the food instead of the food turning below a radiant element. The finish is not the same as you would achieve under a gas grill or electric element, but most people find it acceptable. It is certainly the cleanest grilling method currently available.

Radiant ovens are slow to heat up, wasteful of energy and tend to get dirty in normal use. Most radiant ovens are hotter at the top level than at the bottom but the reverse is true of many European ovens, which have elements above and below instead of at the sides. Radiant cooking gives a special finish to some meat dishes and bread.

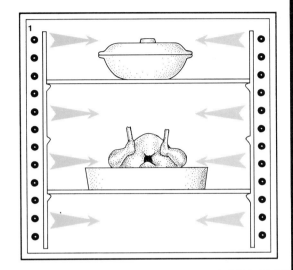

1 Elements

In hot air ovens air is drawn from the oven and blown over a ring element, then back into the cooking space again at several levels. Pre-heating is virtually eliminated and temperatures should be the same at all points. This means you can use every inch for cooking. Ovens no longer have to be big to have adequate cooking capacity. Multi-function ovens combine hot-air cooking with other systems.

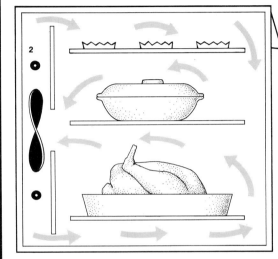

2 Ring elements

Fan-assisted ovens need rather less pre-heating time but, if not self-cleaning, get almost as dirty as radiant ovens and cost almost as much to run. However temperature differences from one part of the oven to another tend to be less so batch cooking is much easier. Some fan-assisted ovens allow for the fan to be switched off if you wish to cook simply by radiant heat to achieve special effects.

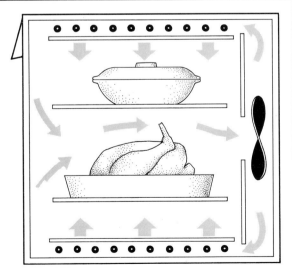

Microwave energy is created in a magnotron and then distributed throughout the cooking space via a "stirrer fan". Some machines cook far more evenly than others but most rely on turntables to equalize the heating effect. The latest microwave cookers also offer hot-air or radiant cooking to increase their all-round usefulness in the kitchen.

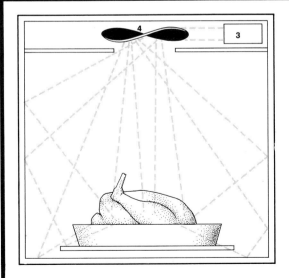

3 Microwave generator
4 Wave distributor

CHOOSING COOKING EQUIPMENT 3

Grills and hobs

In making your final choice of cooking equipment, the extent to which you use a grill and what you use it for will be important factors. If you regularly grill meat and especially if you grill more often than you fry food, it is worth considering the installation of a wall-mounted grilling unit, which may also incorporate a rotisserie.

Proper grilling calls for a very high heat output and therefore the first choice has to be a gas grill. Electric grills, unless they are of the plug-in contact type, and electric grill elements set within ovens are really only browners.

The snag with a gas grill, whether it is wall-mounted or set above a cooker or built-in oven, is that it produces a lot of hot, moist and potentially dirty waste air which can be difficult to extract. The only really satisfactory answer is a commercial-type canopy set well above the grill and incorporating a high power fan. Normal cooker hoods cannot dispose of the large amounts of hot air produced by a gas grill, but as the alternative to proper extraction is an unnecessarily dirty kitchen, the problem is well worth considering carefully to see if your budget will stretch that far.

Depending on what you use a grill for, there are now some interesting alternatives available which may be more satisfactory for your own requirements. For instance, Jenn-Air in America and Gaggenau, Imperial and Miele in Europe offer a built-in electric griddle that sets flush in a worktop and comes with its own downdraught extractor. This will completely dispose of any smoke and flames produced, so long as it can be vented through an adjacent outside wall.

Another alternative, in common use in many countries, is to grill on a griddle plate on the hob. This approach works really well only on a gas hob or a halogen-type ceramic ring, but it is obviously a great deal easier to rinse down a small griddle plate than to clean round a wall-mounted gas grill. A decent extractor cooker hood should be quite capable of dealing with the smoke and steam produced by a griddle plate.

There are several plug-in electric griddles on the market which produce exceptionally good results. As these tend to be quite light, and therefore easy to store away when not in use, they can be a good solution to a tricky problem in a small kitchen.

Slow simmering

Gas has to be the first choice as the fuel for a hob for complete versatility and ease of control, but the very latest ceramic electric hobs, incorporating one or two halogen-type boiling rings, are offering a serious challenge. The point about gas is that it gives you total freedom in your choice of cookwares: if the ability to use flame-proof terracotta pots, a Chinese wok for stir-frying or solid copper pans for flambés or really tricky sauces is important to you, then gas is the only sensible choice of fuel.

Many gas hobs will work on any type of gas. If you do not have a mains supply, bottle gas makes a good alternative. Opt for propane rather than butane as it produces a better flame and is completely odour-free. However, the bottles must be stored outside the house. The latest hobs also tend to be much slimmer, fitting within the thickness of the worktop, so that a drawer can be fitted below them. This, an excellent place to keep often-used utensils, can be important in a small kitchen. Ensure that the hob you choose is fitted either with continuous chromed wire or with "eight finger" pan supports or you may find that small, heavy pots tend to tip over.

The latest electric ceramic hobs, which incorporate a "second generation" type of halogen ring, have developed the cooking-by-light technique to a point at which it offers virtually the same performance as the best gas hobs. The new Imperial hobs, for example, enable you to use just one control setting to bring a pan of milk to the boil and then automatically simmer it without burning or boiling it for as long as your patience lasts. However, you must still use top-quality pans with machined-flat bases on the rest of the rings to be sure of obtaining satisfactory all-round performance in all circumstances.

It is worth remembering that microwave cookers are capable of taking over many of the jobs normally carried out on a hob, such as boiling vegetables, heating liquids and even scrambling eggs. A microwave will also produce superb steamed puddings in just a few minutes. As a microwave is inherently clean (reducing ventilation problems) and may mean that you only need a two-ring gas or electric hob for other purposes, it can be a very attractive as well as a very practical option in a small kitchen.

The best gas hobs have multi-finger pan supports to ensure that, even if a small pot is placed off-centre, it will not topple and spill boiling contents over you or the worktop. In this model, the controls are ideally positioned right at the front and the slimness of the hob allows room for a drawer immediately below. As a fuel, gas frees you to use pans of any material, whereas ceramic and sealed-plate electric hobs need pans with perfectly flat machined metal bases.

Grilling as an alternative to frying is becoming increasingly popular but the problem of how to dispose of the fatty smoke and flames produced by a powerful gas or electric grill has to be solved if your new kitchen furniture is not to be ruined. One answer is to opt for the Gaggenau built-in griddle linked to their powerful downdraught extractor system. The hinged lid at the rear covers the hob completely when it is not in use.

You no longer need a large oven to obtain large-scale cooking capacity. The latest multifunction and hot-air ovens offer the great advantage that every inch of the space inside them can be counted as a practical cooking area, as this view of a fully-loaded ATAG oven shows. This type of oven offers a remarkable range of optional fittings, including two kinds of rotisserie for anything from kebabs to whole chickens.

It is possible to argue that in the smallest kitchens there is no justification for using any form of full-size or built-in cooker at all. The first "cooking package" illustrated on these pages is therefore made up entirely of plug-in equipment.

This basic package would be ideal for a bachelor, a couple who eat out a good deal and entertain only on a small scale, or retired people who are watching capital and running costs carefully. Yet it is remarkably capable and, with a little practice and careful menu planning, could handle dinner parties for six or so without difficulty.

The second package would suit a typical family because it is so flexible that it matches a wide variety of family structures and patterns of living. In any case, it is the essence of family life that living patterns change, often rapidly and unexpectedly, and this package has the advantage of being easy and safe to use, even by people who are unfamiliar with its elements. Note that you have a choice of equipment for several common cooking tasks, such as boiling, casseroling, defrosting, re-heating and plate-warming.

The emphasis in the third package is different because a wall-mounted gas grill and top-quality gas hob have been added to the versatility of a multi-function oven and microwave/hot-air cooker. This combination of equipment is one which suits a wide range of family situations and cookery requirements, especially now that people are getting away from the idea that cooking equipment should be all-gas or all-electric. There is no substitute for gas as a fuel for a grill and a truly versatile hob.

There is also little doubt that the best multi-function electric ovens are so much cleaner, more versatile, compact and cheaper to run than any other variety, that they are now the first choice in most new kitchens. The advantage of using a separate microwave/hot-air cooker, rather than a double oven, is that two people can work at them simultaneously without clashing.

It will take careful planning to incorporate all of the equipment in the eat-in-the-kitchen package into a small kitchen design without sacrificing essential preparation and serving space. If you are really short of space you will be better off with fewer items of specialized cooking equipment in fixed positions. Use easily-moved specialized plug-in gadgets instead because otherwise the kitchen will always be cluttered and hazardous to work in.

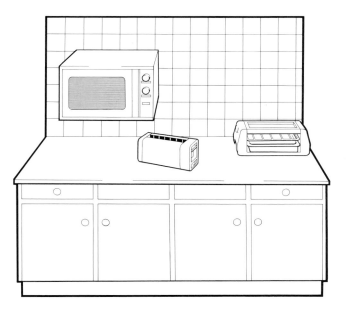

The batchelor package. The heart of this set of cooking equipment is the extra-large Sharp 8320E combined microwave-hot-air oven. Ideally it should be mounted on a wall shelf, leaving the worktop below free for serving. This is backed up by Tefal's snack-maker, which has a small hob surface as well as an internal grill, and the "big slice" toaster by the same company. The microwave handles all boiling, steaming, roasting and baking.

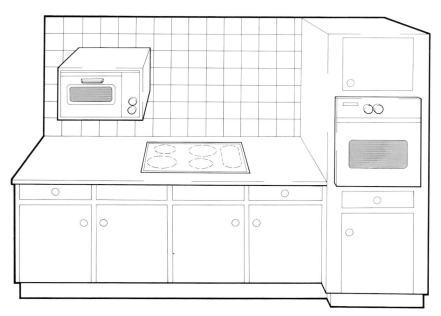

The small family package. A compact arrangement that boasts massive cooking capacity, the main oven is one of the new multi-function single compartment models now offered by many makers which can roast or bake by hot-air or radiant heat and grill by infra-red. To the left a Bosch combined microwave-oven-grill is mounted on the wall for secondary cooking and the inset ceramic hob below has a warming area to the right. This equipment can be arranged so that three could cook without clashing.

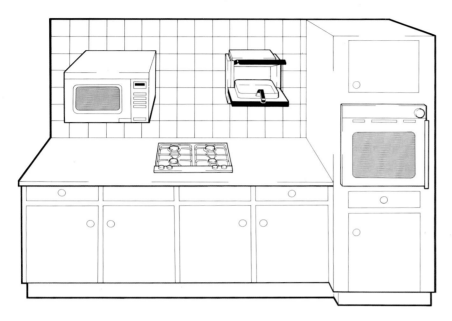

The large family package. Cooking by gas has been added here for greater versatility but the main oven is the remarkable multi-function 700-series model by Gaggenau, which can even be fitted with an electrically-heated "brick" for cooking pizzas in the authentic way. The gas hob shown is also by Gaggenau. Hob cooking by gas has the advantage that you can use a much wider range of pan types. The wall-mounted grill is by Cannon and the combined microwave-hot-air oven by Brother. Care must be taken to site the equipment so that there is working and serving space immediately to hand by every item, however small. Otherwise the advantage of a versatile cooking package such as this will be lost.

The gourmet package. There are three ovens in this setting. The main built-in double oven is by Miele, offering cooking by hot air in one zone and radiant heat in the other, yet in no more total space than a normal Continental oven-and-a-half. The third oven is the Bosch/Siemens combined microwave-oven-grill unit, which is probably the most versatile small-scale cooker on the market. There is a Gaggenau gas hob because gas is a must for specialized cookery and this model has an unusually large top area, which is useful for large pans such as woks or paella dishes. The built-in deep fryer and electric griddle are shown with their own downdraught extractor sited in a centre table or peninsula which may also be used for family meals or even act as the division between the kitchen and dining area.

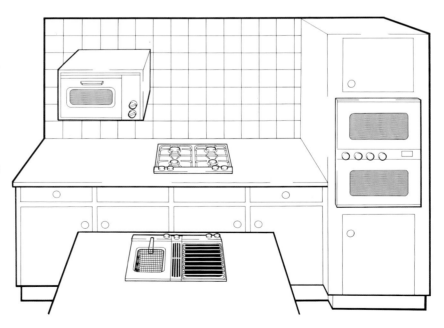

SPACE-SAVING LAYOUTS

Using compact equipment is one way of fitting more cooking facilities into less space, but there are also certain layout ideas that enable you, in effect, to get more use out of a given space. One possibility is to place the cooking area in a corner, with the sink on one side and a pastry-making area on the other. This is a useful way to use a corner that might otherwise tend to be devoted in part to clutter and in part to awkward and inefficient storage.

In this situation an all-in-one cooker (or perhaps a hob and built-under oven) can make some sense. You still take the risk of being caught bending at the oven in the midst of a busy kitchen, but if for structural reasons it is impossible to incorporate a waist-level oven in the design, a corner siting like this can be a solution.

Most cooking hobs are so designed that they have to be set squarely in worktops, which means that you have to work sideways to and from the pans when preparing ingredients or serving. There are quite a few two-burner or two-plate hobs on the market however and though these are relatively expensive they offer some interesting space-saving possibilities.

The diagram below shows how you can employ this idea to get double use out of the worktops in your cooking zone. As you only work on the front half of a worktop, using the back half for the items in immediate use, it is practical to site two-ring hobs in that area. Many people who try this arrangement find that it is more comfortable to work in and out of saucepans, so long as the worktop height is correct, than to have to reach over one pan to get at another on a normal hob.

It will probably pay to create a cooking area like this with worktops slightly deeper than normal, say 26 in. (650 mm) or 28 in. (700 mm) rather than the usual 24 in. (600 mm). Then you can ensure that you have a full 12 in. (300 mm) between the front of the hob and the front of the worktop.

At times when you are not actually using one or all of the hobs, the front space is free for other work. This can be one way to create some pastry-making space in a kitchen which might otherwise appear too small to enable you to do so. Incidentally, setting the hobs at the back of the worktop like this also keeps them well away from small children.

Another version of the same idea is to set hobs in a line down the middle of a peninsula or island. So long as there is a clear 12 in. (300 mm)

between the hobs and the worktop edges on each side – making about 36 in. (900 mm) in all – it will be possible to reach the hobs comfortably from either side for cooking or serving. Such an arrangement also works well as an eating area and it is obviously ideal for table-top cookery, such as stir-frying, Suki Yaki and fondues, because there is plenty of space all around the hob for dinner plates and side dishes of dips and salads.

Another way to get more use out of a given space is to have hobs which disappear when not in use or which are set completely flush into the working surface, without even controls or a surround trim projecting. Some ceramic hobs are made quite specifically to be flush inset like this, so that any part of the surface of the hob which is not hot can be used for anything from preparation to eating. It may sound unsafe, but these hobs have automatic indicators that point out areas that are still warm, even after the ring itself has been switched off.

Alternatively, hobs can be set below the main worktop level and then covered in partly or wholly when you want to use the area for other purposes. Certain makers offer hobs that have drop-down lids of toughened glass or other materials for use as working surfaces when you are not cooking.

Do remember, though, that it is rare in a kitchen to be doing just one thing at a time. The chances are that quite often either you or others will be carrying out several preparatory or cooking tasks simultaneously. This is the beauty of the first two space-saving suggestions, because you can switch at a moment's notice from one task to another without having to lift lids, shift boards or do anything else.

On the other hand, if you have a cooking zone that also has to double as your main dining area, it can be quite useful to have hobs which disappear completely at mealtimes, especially if there is a microwave or multi-function oven close at hand for finishing things off or keeping food warm.

You only use the front half of a worktop for working on, so one way to gain space is to set hobs across the back. The front half is then available for preparation and serving. However, you must ensure that the worktop is not set too high for those using it.

Left: Setting a cooker in the corner is a great space-saving idea for a small kitchen. It often frees worktop space to one side or the other for you to create a proper food-mixing area. Dishes or plates can be set all round the cooktop for serving meals.

This brilliant example of space planning packs more equipment and facilities into a tiny area than you might think possible. The sink is raised slightly to leave space for a dishwasher below and the breakfast bar doubles as a serving zone. A two-ring electric hob is set below the wall-mounted microwave and a chopping board can be fitted into the sink to turn it into a food preparation area. All you need to add is a larder/foodstore and you have a complete kitchen which could even cope with the needs of a small family.

PLUGGING IN TO NEW IDEAS

There is no reason at all why a kitchen has to include a large cooker or a built-in oven and hob in fixed positions. Unless you cook regularly on a large scale, it is now quite practical to equip your kitchen entirely with plug-in appliances. In fact if your kitchen is very small, perhaps sited in one corner of a single-room apartment, this may be the only practical solution. Whatever the reason for your choice, there is now such a wide range of sophisticated plug-in cooking equipment on the market that you need not be limited in the recipes that you tackle.

Several makers offer miniature table-top cookers, many of which combine a small radiant oven with some form of hob top on which you can either cook directly or use normal saucepans. There are also several plug-in portable hot-air ovens now available, such as the Convection Oven by ICTC, which give excellent general-purpose baking and roasting performance.

The big step forward has been the arrival of large-capacity microwave ovens which can also cook by hot air. The best example is the Sharp 8320E, which has an internal capacity of 1½ cu. ft (42.5 cu. dm) and can therefore handle quite large joints of meat with all the trimmings, a really big turkey or several trays of cakes, as well as all the jobs a microwave cooker does so well. These larger-capacity microwave cookers have no more cooking power than their smaller cousins, so it will take longer to cook the larger quantity of food that they are capable of containing. However, you will still find that such ovens cook faster and are cheaper to run than most conventional alternatives.

If you are going to rely entirely on plug-in equipment for all your cooking requirements, it is advisable to choose items that are light enough to handle easily. It is much better to have a large cupboard, perhaps fitted with pull-out shelves or basket drawers, in which all your plug-in appliances can be stored when not in use than to keep them permanently on the worktops. One of the tall cabinets, generally called worktop wall units (as shown on page 61), is excellent for this purpose.

The only machine that you will definitely not want to move often is the microwave cooker which is a key part of a kitchen designed around plug-in equipment. Apart from the fact that all microwave cookers are heavy, even a slight slip in handling may damage the door seals which are essential to safety in operation. It is therefore a good idea to choose a model which has a drop-down door, as this needs less worktop space when open, or to mount this one item permanently on the wall above your main worktop.

It is well worth having several multi-purpose plug-in pans of the type that can be used for frying, boiling, casseroling and roasting, just as you would have a range of pots and pans in an orthodox kitchen, but the real secret of success is to use as many specialized plug-in appliances as possible. Deep-fryers, sandwich-makers, griddles and toasters all have a wide variety of uses in major cookery, far beyond the "snack-making" role to which they are confined in most kitchens.

Unless you cook regularly for more than two or three people, a kitchen equipped entirely with plug-in electrical gadgets is now entirely practical. Machines such as this mini-cooker can roast, bake, grill and brown but also have a hotplate for anything from breakfast-making and griddling snacks to warming plates. Add a straight-forward microwave cooker, a toaster and perhaps an electric fryer and you can handle almost anything.

Plug-in appliances offer a low-cost, compact solution to many kitchen equipment problems but there remains the question of where to put them when they are not in use. This brilliant new range from Black & Decker follows the trend towards fitting plug-ins on walls, under cupboards or on special shelves to keep worktops as clear as possible. The Toast-R-Oven to the left is no bigger than a bread bin yet can bake a 9-inch pie or toast six slices of bread at a time. The big-capacity coffee percolator can be timed to provide a fresh brew when you want it. The Knife Center houses an electric carver with two interchangeable blade types for carving and paring, but also offers space for you to store other specialized cook's knives in a proper hardwood block. Next comes the portable mixer, with five speed settings and storage space for the snap-in attachments. Finally the range is completed by a multipurpose opener for cans, bags and bottles.

SPECIALIZED HOBS

If you carry out certain specific cooking operations frequently enough it may well be worthwhile to install a separate built-in hob designed just for those purposes. Should you be thinking along these lines, consider whether it makes more sense to place all your hobs together or alternatively split them into separate main and secondary groups.

For instance, you might decide to site your main hob at the heart of the primary working area and then set a group made up of a built-in griddle, deep-fryer and twin-cooking hob in a central table or breakfast bar. Special attention will need to be given to planning ventilation and if possible you should incorporate a tiny sink in the layout as well.

Some of these specialized built-in hobs have particular safety or practical advantages compared with the alternative plug-in or on-hob equivalents, so they may well be worth considering on grounds other than simple convenience.

The built-in deep-fryer offered by Gaggenau, Imperial and Miele, for example, has several design features that make it a much better machine than any alternative on the market. The shape of the oil container, the position of the element in the oil, and the handy drain valve in the bottom of the unit all solve practical and safety problems which are common to virtually all other fryers.

The unit is designed in such a way that the oil in use separates naturally from any water that comes out of the food and the element heats the oil rather than the waste and water which accumulate below. This can easily be run off, using the drain valve, leaving the oil clear and untainted for perhaps months at a time. Time after time you can start frying with onion rings in batter and finish with apple rings, without the apple having the slightest trace of other flavours. It sounds like magic but it works.

The American company Jenn-Air, and German makers Gaggenau, Imperial and Miele, offer alternative versions of a built-in electric griddle that vary in certain details. For instance, all these units manage to grill meat with an effect and flavour remarkably like that produced in a charcoal barbecue, though the Jenn-Air cooks over a cast-iron matrix and the other units use substrates of lava rock. In each the underlying system is similar, in that fat from the food being cooked drops onto the iron grid or stone chips and then burns off back onto the steak, chop, sausages, fish or whatever. You can also sprinkle suitable herbs on

the substrate to create specific flavours.

Such griddles should be used only in conjunction with the downdraught extractors that form part of the system or the smoke and smells produced will infiltrate the whole house. In the Jenn-Air version, the griddle and extractor come as a combined unit. Another model by Jenn-Air offers an accompanying plug-in/pull-out hob arrangement, with options of two-place ceramic, radiant electric and other hobs so that you can choose the total combination that suits the meal you have in mind.

Imperial make a range of individual round and oval ceramic hobs that can be inset into a working surface or countertop anywhere you have the need and the space. The control switches come singly, but can be arranged in sets if necessary by the installer and the plates can be fitted either with the normal surround strips or absolutely flush to suit your overall design.

This range of fittings means that it is possible to have a cooking surface of any size and layout installed anywhere you wish, in normal working surfaces, central islands or peninsulas, or even in a dining table or cooking trolley.

Several makers offer modular hob systems that enable you to put together combinations of different types of hobs and other cooking systems to suit special requirements. Some even include a small modular sink in the range and this can save you carrying water to and from a central island or peninsula, so long as the necessary plumbing is practicable.

For those who entertain on a really big scale, these modular hob systems completely solve the problem of creating large cooking areas, but in designing such a setting it is important to ensure that you leave ample space for preparation and serving. Two rules that should be followed whenever possible are that the hobs should be arranged in such a way that there is a clear, heatproof "resting space" at one side of, in front of, or immediately behind every cooking position and that the total serving area immediately around the group of hobs should allow about 1 foot square (300 × 300 mm) for every person who can sit around your dining table for a formal meal.

The point is that whether you are serving directly onto plates, or into dishes that will then be taken to the table, you need this much space to serve a large meal in comfort.

It is a great advantage in a small kitchen to be able to use one surface for a number of purposes. The latest cooking equipment is making this possible in many new situations. Here a ceramic hob has been set flush in a solid maple working surface which doubles as a table. Note how the controls have been set out of the way in a hanging rack above the hob. Even when all four rings are in use, no heat is transmitted into the surrounding woodwork.

Left: The keys to quality deep-frying are clean oil and accurate temperature control. This built-in fryer is constructed in such a way that the oil remains clean and untainted for long periods. This fryer has a timer as well as automatic temperature control. Note also the rack for draining the lift-out baskets before serving. The unit is part of a modular range which incorporates a downdraught extractor and a number of different hobs, including two-ring and four-ring gas, sealed-plate electric and ceramic units which can be installed alone or in groups.

Above: Jenn-Air in America were the pioneers of modular hobs combined with downdraught extractors. Here the right-hand hob unit can be lifted out and replaced with a variety of alternatives for special purposes. These include a radiant electric two-ring set and a powerful electric wok unit which has its own integral steel pan. Built-in griddles like that shown on the left must be used with downdraught extractors to avoid smoke and fumes spreading throughout the entire kitchen if fat or oil catches fire when you are cooking.*

SPECIAL OVENS

In some parts of the world ovens that offer a pyrolitic self-cleaning system – whereby the oven is run at a very high temperature to burn off residues – are commonplace, whereas in other countries their use is rare. The advantage of this system is that it does away with the chore of oven-cleaning completely, at much lower running cost than you might expect. The disadvantage is that the oven needs lots of extra insulation and you therefore have to choose between a bulky machine with a normal-sized oven interior or an appliance of standard size with less than the usual amount of interior space.

Other technical limitations mean that it is difficult to combine a pyrolitic self-cleaning feature with some other cooking systems, such as really sophisticated hot-air roasting and baking or microwave. So you may have to choose one or the other. The only consolation is that the best hot-air ovens and most microwaves (even those in multi-function ovens) stay remarkably clean in normal use so that heavy cleaning is not the regular essential chore that it used to be in the days of radiant ovens.

Generally speaking, gas ovens have not advanced in design as rapidly as electric cookers, mainly because they do not offer the same opportunities for more compact design and electronic controls. The underlying problem presented by any gas oven – and compounded in combined ovens and grills – is that it creates a great deal of hot and probably dirty waste air. There are ways to deal with this problem, as we shall see on page 44. So if you can also cope with the large size of a built-in gas oven and grill, compared with the latest electric alternatives, and if you want the particular finish which only gas cooking can provide, it is worth looking for a machine which offers real advantages in cooking performance, such as TI-New World's current Series Two range. The grill is unique as it utilizes a large matrix burner rather than individual jets and the large oven has been computer designed to feature much less variation in temperature from one part to another than is usual with gas.

Imperial produce a built-in "pressure cooker", that can be bought separately or in combination with one of their multi-function ovens. It is permanently connected to both water and waste services and completely automatic once you have set the cooking time. The machine can also

be used as an automatic steamer without pressure.

This unique appliance is mostly used to cook vegetables, especially dried pulses, which might otherwise take a considerable time. It is also excellent for fast stews and steamed pies and puddings. It is capable of handling many tasks that a microwave can handle, but it is not quite as versatile.

The remarkable Gaggenau 700-series family of ovens offer several unique features to justify their reputation as the ultimate domestic ovens for versatile cooks. In the double-oven versions, you have the option of fitting the grill element in either compartment and also of connecting it in a third socket at the bottom of the main oven. This gives you the special "hotter at the bottom, cooler at the top" cooking conditions essential for certain types of traditional Continental casserole recipes. Alternatively, a ceramic pizza brick can be connected into the same socket, pre-heated and then used to cook half a dozen or so pizzas or perhaps even nan bread or chappatis.

These features are additional to the usual multi-function cooking system which we now take for granted in the best Continental ovens. If you wish, you can order any model with built-in extraction, so that absolutely no air or smells from the oven are recirculated to the kitchen. Should you be planning to combine your kitchen with your dining room, or perhaps even site it at one end of a living area, that can be a crucial advantage. Gaggenau's supremely elegant styling is another.

Gaggenau's 700-series ovens offer a wide range of special features and extras. Here the accessory pizza brick is shown on which, after pre-heating, pizzas can be cooked in the authentic way. The brick can also be used for Eastern breads and other types of baking. The second oven in this version is in fact a microwave cooker, but an orthodox small oven and grill can be ordered instead if you wish. Another option is an integral oven extractor which collects all cooking fumes and ducts them right out of the kitchen.

Computer design techniques were employed during the development of this New World gas oven. As a result, mixed cooking and intensive use of space are possible as in the best electric hot-air and multi-function alternatives. However, this oven has the advantage of a very high-performance gas grill, housed in a second compartment above. In one version this area can also be used as a second oven or warming area.

Below: Makers Imperial offer three alternatives for fitting above their main built-in multi-function oven: a smaller secondary oven and grill; a sophisticated microwave cooker with meat-probe heat control; and the built-in pressure cooker, with a convenient swing-up door, shown here. The microwave and pressure cooker can be bought as separate items and could be set in a different part of the kitchen from the main oven.

REFRIGERATION

However small a kitchen may be, it is a mistake to be mean about the size of your fridge and freezer. Think of them as storage space and approach your choice of equipment using the same criteria you would apply to cupboards or a larder.

The latest models increasingly make use of pull-out shelves and baskets, to maximize internal space and to make everything the unit contains much more accessible. When space is severely limited, build in your fridge at waist level with cupboard space above and below for items you rarely need, or consider fitting one of the latest roll-out models below a working surface.

The trend in the best equipment is towards adaptable multi-zone refrigerator/freezer/chillers. These machines are divided into three compartments – one for freezing, one for normal refrigeration and one which operates at a higher "cellar" temperature. This last section is valuable for chilling wine and for keeping salads crisp, soft cheeses in perfect condition and cold dishes just table-ready. In most of these machines you can easily adjust how much space is given to refrigeration and how much to chilling, or switch both areas to refrigeration to meet special requirements.

American machines are often even more sophisticated, though they are generally much larger and sometimes quite difficult to integrate into a really small room. However, most offer some important advantages such as completely automatic defrosting of the freezer and built-in dispensers for ice and cold drinks.

The White Westinghouse RS26VG (seen on the far right) is a good example of how large fridges now contain useful specialized facilities for food storage and even aids to preparation. The upper of the two pull-out trays at the bottom of the right-hand section is a chilled meat compartment in which large amounts of fresh meat can be kept in perfect condition for up to a week as an alternative to freezing. It has an impressive capacity of up to 2 cu. ft (57 cu. dm). The chilling effect is achieved by continually circulating cold air round the outside of the container but not through it, so that the contents are not dried. The space can also be converted when required for chilled storage of fresh fruit and vegetables at a somewhat higher temperature.

In the same machine, the internal cabinet at the top on the right is a special compartment for chilling down jellies or cooked foods quickly without

drying them out. When not required for this purpose it can be converted for normal refrigeration. The existence of specialized facilities like these can be of considerable value when attempting large-scale cookery in a small kitchen, even if the requirement is only occasionally needed.

The noise a refrigerator makes becomes important in a small space. If possible, listen to the model you are considering buying, preferably to one that has been installed and operating for some time. There is nothing more irritating than the noise of a fridge motor cutting in and out in an otherwise quiet room, especially if the space is shared with your dining or perhaps your main living area.

Built-in fridges are now available in two categories. Some can be fitted with decor panels – sheets of either plastic laminate or veneered plywood – so that they more or less match the adjoining furniture. Others are described as integrated, which means they are designed to disappear entirely behind complete cabinet doors. The internal capacity of integrated models is slightly less when related to the space they occupy, but the fact that they are hidden behind doors means that not only do they fit in with the rest of the kitchen visually, but compressor noise is completely masked.

This integrated fridge by Neff has three storage zones: a three-star freezer at the top; refrigeration in the centre; and chilling space below the divider. You can adjust the proportions of fridge and chilling space or have refrigeration throughout when you require it.

Left: The giant three-zone freezer/fridge/chiller by AEG-Telefunken packs a huge amount of storage space into a space only 3 ft by 2 ft (900 x 600 mm). The chiller space below can be converted into an additional refrigeration area at the turn of a switch if you suddenly need more capacity.

Above: White Westinghouse's huge multi-zone refrigerated foodstore has many special facilities such as dispensers for ice and chilled water; frost-free freezing as well as refrigeration; chillers for fresh meat as well as hot foods which you need to cool in a hurry; and lots of general-purpose space.

TUCKAWAY APPLIANCES 1

There are two main reasons for hiding a piece of equipment away. The first is that it may enable you to use what might otherwise be wasted space, such as a corner. The second is that, if the room is also a living area, you may want equipment or fittings to be invisible when you are not actually using them.

Most makers of kitchen appliances now offer many models that either hide away behind panels which exactly match the furniture or come in toning colour finishes. It is also worth noting that such machines are often inherently quiet as well, thanks in part to the extra sound insulation provided by a heavy door panel. So integrated dishwashers and laundry equipment may well be worth considering for that reason alone.

Considerable economies in space are now possible with laundering equipment, thanks to the development of combined washer/dryers, some of which can be pre-set to carry out the whole process without interruption. Many of these machines dry laundry without the need for external ducting, by condensing out the steam and pumping it away with the rest of the waste water. Now that low-temperature detergents are in common use, the argument in favour of cold-feed-only laundering machines is unanswerable, so we now have super-compact washer/dryers that require only a cold feed, a waste outlet and electricity.

Combined washer/dryers wash larger loads than they dry. Heavy users found this a disadvantage because they had constantly to reduce the load between washing and drying.

However, the new generation of machines is so economical on half-load settings that it now pays to sort your laundry into smaller, specialized loads.

The disposal of waste, always a problem in a small kitchen, is made easier by electric waste compactors, which will press tins, jars, boxes and any other rubbish you wish to be rid of into plastic-wrapped cubes, much reducing the number of trips you have to make to the dustbin.

The single tiny bins so often fitted below kitchen sinks cannot be described as labour saving, partly because they are hardly capable of holding a day's total rubbish, but also because they do not enable you to discriminate between types of waste.

If you are a keen gardener, you will probably want to keep food scraps aside for your compost heap with another bin devoted to dustbin rubbish. Even in the limited space below a double-bowl system sink there is adequate space for two quite large bins, such as the 15-litre Big Box made by Hailo. The same company makes much larger bins which can be housed in a cupboard below your worktop and reached through a trapdoor or lift-out chopping block. This bin is big enough to take a full-size dustbin liner, yet the split lid seals very effectively, so you can use it as a means of reducing the number of times you have to make the journey to your dustbin. The latest bin fittings incorporate two tall, square, but relatively narrow bins, sharing a snap-down cover when closed and sliding out together for easy access as you open the cupboard door.

Roll-out larder fridges are now offered by several makers. In this version by Imperial there is a handy bottle store at the front of the bottom tray and this entire tray lifts out for cleaning. The two see-through baskets above have a huge potential capacity. This type of fridge is not a direct equivalent to an orthodox model but it makes an excellent chilled foodstore. Other models offer more conventional refrigerated storage and freezer versions are also available.

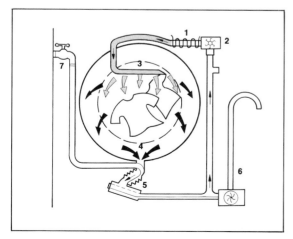

Laundry dryers no longer need to be ducted out through a wall. The latest machines condense the steam, pump it to waste and re-use the hot air, cutting running costs considerably. This diagram of the AEG-Telefunken condenser dryer system shows how cold water from the mains is used to cool the moist air once it has passed through the drum. The air then returns through a small blower unit and a heater to the top of the drum again. This system means that combined washer-dryers only need a cold water input, a drainage connection and a normal power circuit.

1 AIR HEATER
2 FAN
3 FRESH HOT AIR
4 MOIST AIR
5 CONDENSER
6 WASTE WATER PIPE
7 COLD WATER SUPPLY

The latest generation of dishwashers will handle anything from dirty saucepans to lead crystal glass, if you set the correct programme. But just as important for most people, they are quieter and much less visually obtrusive. This fully integrated model is designed to be fitted with a solid-wood cabinet door to match the surrounding cupboards rather than the familiar decor panel. The visual advantages are obvious but the fitting of this solid panel also cuts noise, so that the machine is virtually silent when operating. Fully-integrated dishwashers like this are fixed permanently into the surrounding cabinets and are designed not to be removed again till the end of their life. All servicing and replacement of parts take place from the front. A wide range of alternative control panel facias are available for this model to enable the designer to match it closely with the chosen kitchen colour scheme.

If you are not retaining food scraps for your compost heap it is well worth considering a waste disposer in your sink. Few people who have once owned a disposer would consider doing without one in their next kitchen. There are two basic types: the batch-feed model in which you fill a container and then switch on the grinder by fitting and turning the waste plug; and the continuous-feed type which you switch on to grind and then add as much waste as you like while running the tap to wash the chopped-up remains away.

It is sometimes suggested that the batch-feed models are safer, as you cannot reach into the area where the cutters are sited when they are turning. However, most people buy continuous-feed disposers and, apart from consuming the odd spoon, both types appear to give long and totally reliable service.

Most problems with disposers arise from installing the cheaper versions which have motors that are too small to handle some commonplace kitchen waste items, such as tough sweet-corn cores. It is a false economy to buy a cheap disposer. Choose one which has good sound insulation, is self-sharpening and auto-reversing and has a motor of at least $\frac{1}{2}$ horsepower.

If there is space in your kitchen, or you are incorporating a central island or multi-purpose peninsula for both working and eating in the design, consider fitting a small sink with a waste disposer in the island. You may also decide to site the dishwasher there, ready for dirty plates from the breakfast area or when brought through from the dining room.

The sink can be covered in with a wood board when not in use and the advantage of this approach is that you can plan for dishwashing and china storage outside the main food preparation area. You might also decide to place a small hob or perhaps a built-in deep-fryer and griddle next to the small sink, creating a completely self-contained secondary cooking area for snacks and other informal meals.

Food processors and mixers pose one of the most difficult space planning problems. If they are to be really useful they must be readily to hand; unless they are to be continually in view on the worktop there are only two possible solutions. The first is to house them in a special cupboard, with a roller shutter door, in which they stay continually plugged in but always ready to disappear. The second is to use a Nutone Food Center.

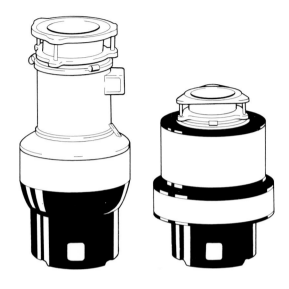

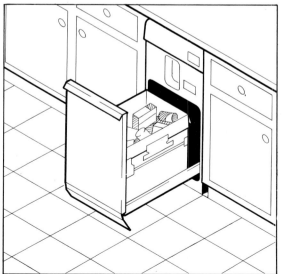

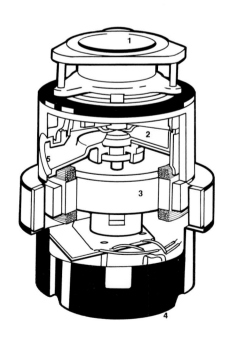

When pulled out, this trash compactor looks much like a normal waste bin. Push it in and a power-driven ram descends to crush the waste into a fraction of the space it would normally occupy. Though compactors handle food scraps and wet waste happily enough, they are ideal for bulky cartons, non-returnable bottles and cans. This model fits into the same space as a standard waste bin.

Waste disposal units are taken for granted in America and rapidly gaining popularity in Europe. These diagrams show the batch-feed model above left and the continuous-feed above right. Apart from the extra top chamber on the batch-feed model, both types are technically similar. Bottom: a specially-designed connector (1) makes fitting to an appropriate sink simple. The top chamber (2) contains the cutters which, in the better quality models, reverse direction each time the machine is switched off and on again. The drive motor is immediately below (3) which, for complete reliability, should be ½ horsepower. At the base is the control system (4), containing the anti-jam mechanism and automatic reverse system. The waste outlet (5) can be connected simply to most undersink systems. Some machines also have a connection for the drain outlet from your dishwasher, so collected scraps will be ground up the next time the dispenser is used.

This excellent machine comprises a built-in motor unit with variable-speed control plus a wide range of plug-in gadgets, which can be stored in a basket, a drawer below the worktop that has been suitably divided up, or on Nutone's two-tier accessory rack which can be fitted into almost any base cupboard and takes the whole range of fittings. The motor unit is set virtually flush in a worktop, probably just off-centre in the main working area, ideally between the sink and pastry-making slab.

Nutone's wide range of snap-in accessories cover almost every conceivable food preparation requirement, plus such interesting additions as an ice crusher, knife sharpener and can opener. The blender-liquidizer has a large capacity and a lid constructed to enable you to add oils safely. The fact that the unit can be switched on or off at any pre-set speed and the speed varied as you go is particularly useful when making mayonnaise or liquidizing home-made soups. There is a food processor attachment, but keen cooks will particularly welcome the mincer, shredder and slicer fittings. These enable you to create a series of elements for a salad, for instance, without the usual problem of repeatedly cleaning out a food processor bowl. The range is completed by a series of juicers for particular purposes, mixers and even special fittings for use in making baby food.

Among the most difficult items to store satisfactorily in any kitchen are food mixers and processors. If they are not kept readily to hand their usefulness is limited, yet there is nothing that clutters up a working surface more than a food mixer which is not being used. One of the best answers to this problem is the Nutone Food Center system above. By no means a new product, the Nutone system has established an enviable reputation for robust quality and reliability.

However small your kitchen may be, don't save space by skimping on the most-used item of equipment it contains – the sink. If you think that having a dishwasher means that you need only a small sink for food preparation, and perhaps rinsing out mixing bowls and breakfast china, think again. The realities of working in a family kitchen prove otherwise.

The trick is not to choose a small sink, which is useless for practically every purpose, but to go for a big one which can be adapted to dozens of different jobs. In other words, choose a sink to suit the largest items you may wish to fit into it and then ensure that it can easily be adapted to small jobs.

The first of the current generation of system sinks was the Franke Compact. This brilliant three-bowl design in satin-finished stainless steel is still one of the best available, but the key to its real value is the range of accessories which adapt it to particular tasks. A wood block turns either sink into a working surface. A strainer basket for the centre bowl doubles as a colander. There is a draining basket and a drop-in draining board as well. If you plan your under-sink space carefully, you should be able to store such items there when they are not required for use.

An alternative approach is to install a really big single sink – say, a Victorian china bowl – and to adapt it for smaller jobs with a made-to-measure chopping board which fits on top and a plastic bowl from your local hardware store. This way you achieve many of the advantages of the latest system sinks at a fraction of the cost. However, do ensure that you buy a genuine Victorian bowl, about six inches (150 mm) deep, as modern versions are much deeper and will give you backache.

A modern big sink is offered by Kohler. Their Mayfield model is a real giant. You can order the same company's 1½-bowl Lakefield with a fitted chopping board. These sinks also follow another trend in that they can be installed flush with the surrounding working surface, so that water and scraps can be wiped straight off the top into the sink. Kohler make their bowls of enamelled cast iron, which is more resistant to damage than enamelled steel.

Imperial offer a wide range of sinks on porcelain-finished fireclay, which are totally modern in concept even though they recall the traditions of a century ago in the material used.

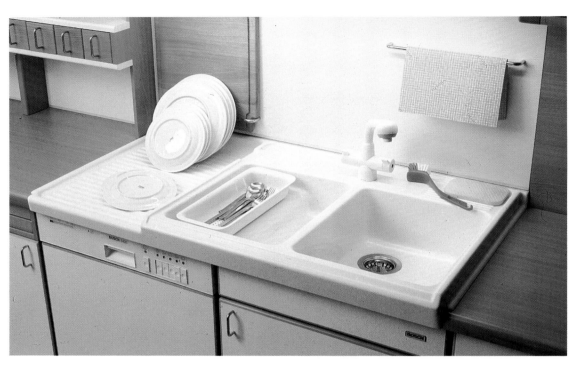

Among the new generation of system sinks, the Bosch double sink shown here has been designed specifically to be used in association with a dishwasher, with the base of the left-hand bowl profiled to fit round the machine below. The taps incorporate a pull-out spray rinse head and are now available to fit most types of plumbing system. Despite the dishwasher below, the sink is shown set out for washing up because it is now widely accepted, even by makers of dishwashers, that most people will choose to deal with small quantities of crockery by hand rather than wait to build up a full load in the machine. Now that the 1970s' vogue for small round sink bowls is outdated, most makers have reverted to the far more practical oblong bowl shape. They have also realized that it is much more useful to have a wide bowl than a deep one, especially when washing up oven shelves or large baking trays.

The double sink has now been converted into a food preparation area. One of the bowls has disappeared and a fitted chopping board has been lifted down from the rack to the left where it was hanging during washing up. The block could just as easily have been set above the large sink to the right, with the small cutlery draining basket shown in the picture on the left used in this case as a colander. The rinsing head can now be used to clean vegetables. A waste disposer would have to be fitted in the right-hand bowl, because the presence of the dishwasher to the left means that there is not adequate space for it on that side.

Sink systems of such complex design as this are possible only because many exciting new materials are now available. This model is in Asterite by ICI, a tough plastic which looks like porcelain, but resists accidental damage and is quieter to use than sinks made of stainless or enamelled steel.

Even in a small kitchen use of traditional china sinks can be an excellent idea, especially if you also have a large wooden draining rack. Care should be taken to ensure that you use a sink of the proper depth. When set below a wood worktop as here, the inside of the sinks should not be more than six inches (150 mm) deep or you will almost certainly suffer backache in time. These shallow sinks are not easy to find, but beware of using laboratory sinks instead, which are usually much too deep for comfort.

NEW VIEWS ON SINKS 2

Villeroy & Boch market system sinks in both ceramics and the latest man-made materials and they have taken system-sink thinking yet a stage further with their Pallas designs. In effect you have a main sink bowl which can be varied in size according to the task in hand, though the centre position will usually be occupied by either a small accessory bowl or a strainer. If you opt for the version with the centre waste, this can in effect be used as an ''overflow'' if you are preparing vegetables in running water in the deeper part.

The space-saving advantages of corner working arrangements, already discussed on page 24 in relation to hobs, can be adopted for sinks. Both Villeroy & Boch and Imperial have developed models that exploit this design concept, though in fact virtually any sink can be installed in this way. However, both the specialized corner sinks do offer certain design advantages.

Villeroy & Boch's Venue model uses the same variable-size main bowl idea as their Pallas sink, though with different geometry. Imperial's version has somewhat smaller bowls, but the clever surround rim does solve the problem of how to contain water in the sink area completely while also creating safe resting places for hot pans or items which are wet or dirty.

Many sink mixer taps are now fitted with ceramic valves instead of washers. Once correctly installed, such taps need only a quarter-turn from full on to off and should give indefinite drip-free service. Single-lever taps are also becoming commonplace, though drinking water safety regulations limit their use in some countries.

An interesting recent development is the hot water dispenser. Models available can guarantee enough boiling water instantly for anything from 40 to 100 cups of tea or coffee an hour. If you have one throw your kettle away and save space.

Detergent dispensers are now commonplace. They may not save much space, but they do eliminate the need to bend for the bottle of washing up liquid every time you need some.

Many companies now offer pull-out hot-rinse sprays, but it is worth thinking carefully about how you would use one before having it fitted. All dishwasher makers recommend that any pre-rinsing is done with cold water, to avoid sealing food onto plates or pans. You may therefore consider a cold spray, useful for rinsing vegetables and salads as well, a better idea.

Above: If you have a big cooker you need a big sink in which to soak oven shelves and tins. It is therefore hardly surprising that American makers offer the biggest sinks on the market and that they tend to be exceptionally durable. This double-bowl model is made of enamelled cast iron. Note the drop-in draining rack being used here during vegetable preparation.

Right: Villeroy & Boch make ceramic sinks in a wide variety of shapes and sizes, some of which offer striking design possibilities. The unusual twin-bowl model shown here is designed to be set flush into a laminate-covered worktop. The plastic surface actually runs over the edge of the outer rim so that water spilt from the sink can be wiped straight back into one of the bowls.

Other sinks in this range are designed to fit into diagonal corners and a number of other difficult locations. They are made of both ceramic materials and Asterite, and are designed for flush insetting into tiled, stone or hardwood worktops. Most are offered with a complete range of fitted chopping blocks, draining racks, drop-in secondary bowls and colanders.

LIGHTING

The lighting you choose for your kitchen will play as important a role in creating the total atmosphere of the room as the colour scheme, your choice of furniture or even the basic layout. The reason is that light affects everything. As many hours in every kitchen are spent working by artificial light, creating a proper lighting plan is essential.

The rules for creating a successful lighting scheme are, mercifully, simple – throw light exactly where it is required but, unless the fitting is a design feature, ensure that its source is invisible.

Artificial light has two jobs to do in the kitchen. It enables you to work safely at all times and it helps to define the size, shape and colour of the room and its contents. It is often useful to tackle these two aspects of light separately and to create a scheme that will enable you to adapt to changing requirements.

Lights should be placed immediately above working areas, but carefully positioned and baffled to ensure that glare will not reach you directly or indirectly. The worst arrangement for working light in a kitchen is a fluorescent strip placed on the ceiling in the middle of the room. If you have a light like this, wait until it gets dark and then try a simple experiment.

Stand where you can see both the light fitting and a main working area, perhaps the sink, or your cooker or hob. Now hold a magazine or large piece of thick paper in such a way that it obscures the light, but still enables you to see the sink. You will notice that the working area now looks lighter. The reason is that if the source of the light is visible, your eye will respond to this area of maximum brightness and everything else will appear darker than it is. Hide the bright light source and your eye responds by seeing greater brightness elsewhere.

Centre lighting is therefore the worst possible solution in almost every small kitchen, unless you have a combined kitchen and dining area. If so, you may wish to use a pendant or rise-and-fall lamp above the eating area. Another possibility would be to use downlighters, but ensure that the type you choose are those described as "darklighters", in which the source is either invisible or has very low brightness. Whatever your choice, make sure that this central light can be switched off when it is not specifically required.

Generally speaking, working lights will be fluorescent strips fitted below shelves or wall cupboards. Make sure that the tubes used produce the right colour. The best are the ultra-warm white types such as Sylvania Homelight de Luxe. They have very low glare and give the room and the food you are preparing the same warm appearance as you achieve with normal light bulbs, but without the heat and high running cost.

This need for concealed strip lighting above working areas, including the sink, may make it necessary to adapt your furnishing plans. The same is true of the room's background lighting. Often the best way to create this is to hide warm white fluorescent strips above wall cabinets or tall cupboards, creating areas of pooled light which bounce off the ceiling out into the room.

This technique always has the effect of making a room appear larger, but remember that the quality of the light created will depend on the surfaces from which it is reflected. For instance, light bouncing off a glossy white ceiling will appear relatively bright, whereas if it is reflected off dark wood little of it will emerge to light the kitchen itself.

It is worth ensuring that your working and background lighting are switched separately, so that you can vary the amount and distribution of light in the kitchen according to what you are doing. Once you have satisfied the basic requirement for task and background lighting, additional lights may well be used decoratively and as design elements in their own right. However, this is an area for specialists and you should ensure that the practical needs of your kitchen are never forgotten in the creation of special effects.

Left: This kitchen has been filled with light, yet the sources are entirely concealed. As the eye is not aware of the bright source you need less powerful lighting to achieve the levels required for safe working. The light bounced off the ceiling is quite sufficient in a white room to provide perfectly adequate background illumination in the double sink area opposite.

Above: Clever siting of the task lighting near the sink means that it is invisible to the person working there yet gives them more than enough direct illumination for safety. Directing light just where you need it is much better than attempting to flood the whole room with an even blanket of light. Plan switching to enable you to change lighting to suit mood and use.

VENTILATION

Ventilation is even more important in small kitchens than in larger rooms. If you wish your kitchen to share space with your dining area, or even your main living room, close attention to well-planned ventilation is the only thing that will save you from some unpleasant consequences. The main result of not ventilating your kitchen properly is, to put it bluntly, dirt everywhere.

It is surprising how often people who are fastidious and hygiene-conscious will neglect proper ventilation. Today's double-glazed, draught-free houses pose special problems. Only positive planning will enable you to avoid the kind of kitchen that provides bacteria – and some of their larger colleagues – with moist, dark corners to breed in.

The key is regular changes of the air in the kitchen area and this means making provision for fresh air to enter as well as for soiled air to leave. Don't depend on drawing air for your extractor from adjoining rooms, because that simply means that you are throwing away money on your central heating.

A recirculating cooker hood will not solve the problem. What you need is a system which will take soiled air, together with the moisture and dirt which it contains, and pass it right out of the house. Using a recirculating charcoal cooker hood is rather like spraying your vegetable waste with deodorant and then leaving it in a bin to rot.

However, the main problem is that dirt in the kitchen is closely associated with the moisture that most cooking processes produce, especially if you use gas for a hob, oven or grill. If this moist air is not collected and disposed of, the dirt has to go somewhere – so it coats decorations, shelves, cupboards and anything else that is exposed, not to mention the carpets and soft furnishings in a cooking/eating/living area.

To achieve adequate levels of ventilation, the air in a kitchen area has to be totally replaced at least three times every hour. That does not mean a howling gale. It can be achieved in almost total silence with the proper planning and equipment.

Fitting a powerful cooker hood is not the answer, because moisture and smells are produced in many places other than above the hob. In any case, that does not solve the problem of bringing fresh air into the kitchen and without that your extractors will not work satisfactorily anyway.

The ideal solution is a ventilated larder with

fresh air introduced at the base, passing through the interior and out through a grille at the top, across the ceiling and then out of the room through a main extractor. In small rooms it may be sufficient to rely on the extractor to draw the air it needs through the larder; this will work as long as the size of the intake duct to the larder is somewhat larger than the duct out from the cooker hood.

If you have a larger space, or your kitchen shares a room with the eating or living area, more precise arrangements will have to be made. The fresh air intake to the larder (or perhaps to a vegetable store below a worktop) should be fitted with its own fan, controlled by the same switch that operates the extractor system. Whenever you switch on the extractor the whole room will benefit; and the extractor system itself becomes twice as effective. In other words, for a given extraction effect the cooker hood will probably need to work at only half the speed.

If your kitchen occupies one part of a much larger room, ensure that the flow of air from your larder intake does not cross the eating area to reach the extractor. You may well have a downdraught extractor system serving a built-in deep-fryer, a barbecue, or a hob set into the surface of a table at which you also eat. If so, make sure that enough air enters the kitchen to balance both the downdraught extractor and a high-level ventilation unit placed elsewhere. The first will deal with smoke and steam produced at the hob, but the second is essential to ensure that more general fug is drawn away from the eating and living areas.

Several makers are now producing sophisticated solutions to particular ventilation problems. The Swedish company Futura make a cooker hood that creates its own intake airflow by supplying a curtain of fresh air around the hob through downward jets. Gaggenau offer a version of some of their ovens with a built-in extractor system, venting all cooking smells, steam and smoke directly to the outside of the house.

Most extractor systems designed for use above hobs or ovens contain grease filters, to reduce the deposition of fat on the inside of the air duct through the wall. The best of these are now entirely of stainless steel mesh, so that they can be cleaned regularly in the sink or dishwasher. Futura extractors employ a maze of plastic fingers, upon which moist soil is deposited as the air passes through. This whole section can be lifted out easily

Forget about noisy, space-consuming cooker hoods; as this example by Bulthaup shows, extractors are now being designed to integrate far better into modern kitchen styling and to do their work without robbing you of space in key areas. You pull out the see-through acrylic shield when you wish to use the extractor. All the works are hidden behind the useful box drawers and shelves above.

for regular washing, completely removing the need to search for replacement filter elements.

Don't allow the fact that your cooker is not conveniently sited on an outside wall to excuse poor ventilation planning. Any skilled designer will be able to solve this problem easily: there is now a wide range of extractor ducting systems, including booster fans for long runs, to overcome the most difficult situations.

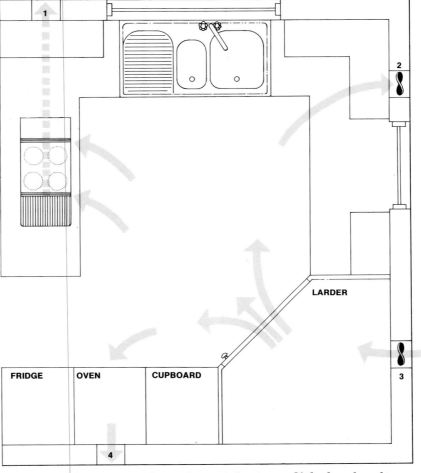

1. Downdraught extractor system in modular hob arrangement.
2. High-level wall extractor fan
3. Low-level fan
4. Integral oven fume extractor

LARDER

FRIDGE | OVEN | CUPBOARD

Above: It is as vital to plan for a good supply of fresh air into the kitchen area as it is to ensure that stale, dirty air is quickly extracted. One way to do this is to site the intake for fresh air in your larder. This will ensure that every time you use the extractor, the larder is ventilated as well.

You will also find that the extractor works far better, which means that you can use it effectively at lower speeds, which in turn means less noise. Try to arrange for the fresh air to enter the larder at low level and pass out into the kitchen at high level. This will ensure that you are free of draughts and that any stale air up near the ceiling is skimmed off in the process.

Apart from the fact that a properly ventilated kitchen is more comfortable to work in (and insures that smells are not transmitted to the rest of the house), it will also need springcleaning far less frequently.

This more elaborate ventilation plan might apply to a kitchen which shares a room with an eating or living area. Again the fresh air enters through the larder at low level but in this case a fan (3) is wired to draw air in every time any of the three extractor systems comes into operation. A skilled electrician can arrange for a relay control to increase the throughput of this intake fan according to the number of extractors running.

This is essential in the case of the twin downdraught extractors which form part of the modular hob arrangement, as otherwise they will be fighting for the available air and will therefore be less effective.

If the downdraught extractors are to whisk away smoke and flames from the griddle on the left satisfactorily, an adequate supply of fresh intake air is essential. In such a room arrangement it is always a good idea to have a high-level extractor fan on the side of the kitchen opposite to the dining or living area, just to use at times when there is a lot of food preparation activity going on. There are several ovens available now which contain their own extractor systems, and in some of these it is even possible to grill meats behind a closed door. With a total system like this there is no reason why cooking smells need ever pass out of the kitchen area.

SERVICES

In looking for ways to save space it pays to plan the areas you cannot see just as carefully as those you can. In many kitchens a good deal of space within cabinets is wasted because water and waste pipes, waste traps, and soil drains from rooms above intrude into the carefully-planned cupboards.

Try to run as few pipes as possible through cupboard interiors. To achieve this, either set the cupboards forward an inch or two, with the worktops extended over the gap at the back, so that pipes can be run in the space created, or run all your pipes in the otherwise wasted plinth space.

The second method is the ideal but there may be technical reasons why it cannot be done. Many makers now design cabinets with a "working void" at the back as a standard feature.

Space immediately below the sink itself is often wasted, especially if you have chosen one of the new multi-outlet system sinks. If orthodox plumbing fittings are used, the space becomes cluttered with a mass of pipes and traps, leaving little space for other essentials such as waste bins, cleaning materials and a utility bucket.

The new type of waste outlet and trap system shown takes all the pipework direct to the back wall and then down to one trap. Local regulations in some areas may prevent you using this system, but it is a marvellous space-saver.

There are always problems in heating kitchens, mainly because heat is often needed when the rest of the house is not in use or because when the central heating is full on the kitchen is too hot. The answer is to treat the kitchen as a separate area, either by fitting local thermostats to the kitchen branch of the radiator system or by fitting special floor-level heaters into the base of a couple of cupboards.

Two types of plinth heater are available, working either off the normal central heating circuit or incorporating electrical elements. In both, the fans operate only when heat is required and that heat is blown just where you want it – across the floor and onto your feet.

Once you have decided where to site plug-in equipment, make sure that electrical outlets are fitted as close as possible to where they are needed. Then you can shorten the cables fitted to your mixer, food processor, griddle, sandwich-toaster, coffee grinder or kettle to the length they need to be. This is a great contribution to both safety and space-saving.

Make sure that electric outlets are placed high enough to be clearly visible and accessible when the worktop is in use and cluttered with other items. Setting sockets high up like this also ensures that you do not waste part of your working area by covering it with coils of cable.

If the kitchen is being extensively renovated it will probably make sense to replace the whole of the electrical wiring system. The best way to do this is to have a high-capacity cable brought from your main consumer unit (where the meter is) through to a big cupboard in which can be fitted a smaller consumer unit covering all kitchen requirements.

This new unit could contain fuses but it probably makes more sense to opt for the newer miniature circuit breakers. These work on the principle that if a problem occurs with any item of electrical equipment in the kitchen, the circuit breaker covering that appliance will trip out but the rest of the equipment will still be connected and working.

One large circuit breaker covers the whole unit, so that everything can be switched off at one point if necessary. It is also easy to isolate any specific appliance for servicing. An expert is necessary to design such a unit but once installed it should be trouble-free and much easier to deal with than a whole battery of fuses.

Most circuit breakers can be labelled, allowing you to identify which piece of equipment is covered by each. When they are tripped by a breakdown or overload, a red indicator shows which one has "blown". All that is then required is to cure the fault and then push the breaker switch back to "on". No wires or cartridges need to be replaced.

Another useful development is the high pressure hot water system. In older houses in which the position of the kitchen sink may have been altered several times over the years, the hot water pressure is often not satisfactory. It is now possible under rules recently approved to fit an electric water heater below the sink or in a convenient cupboard and connect this direct to the mains. Again, such a system requires expert design but it does save long runs of piping from an existing roof tank.

High pressure systems like this formerly required special taps but it is now possible to use them with any design. However, these should still have National Water Council approval for complete safety.

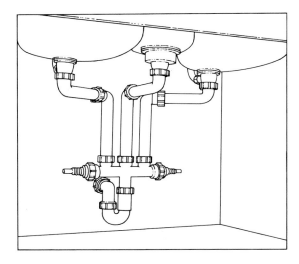

The space below sinks, especially the new multi-bowl models with several outlets, is often cluttered with pipes and waste traps. Several makers now offer special waste kits which take the pipes straight back to the wall and a single shared trap, leaving most of the space free for bins and other storage. Note that in this case there are also connectors for a dishwasher and washing machine. Alternative kits are available for every type of sink and also for waste disposers.

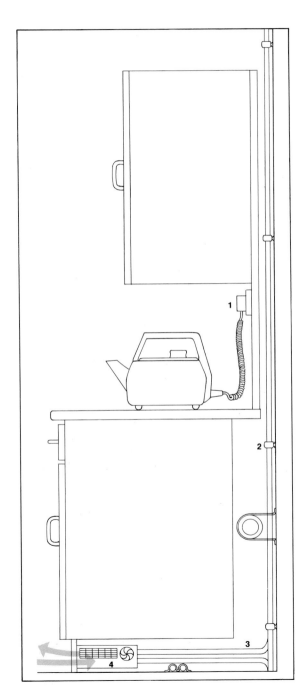

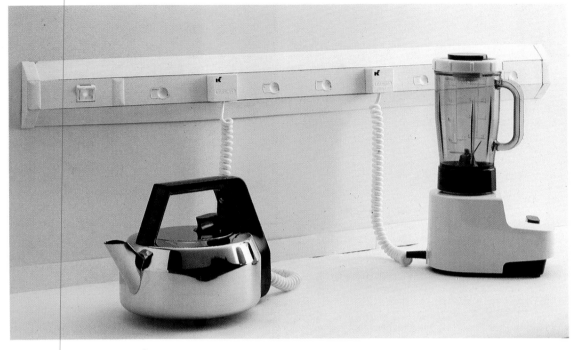

1 High-level sockets keep wires off worktops
2 Void carries waste and central heating pipes
3 Hot and cold water pipes laid in plinth area
4 Plinth heater connected to central heating

Left: If your kitchen is full of awkward pipe runs, set cupboards forward slightly to allow the pipes to run behind rather than cut into the cupboards. Overall there will be no loss of useful space. Even in a small kitchen it can pay to set base cupboards forward under an extra-deep worktop to make a service space for drains. The extra space is particularly useful around sinks and hobs in any case. Run water pipes at floor level, site room heaters in plinths and set power points up under cupboards.

Above: The Kenwood International Electrack system means that you can have power for electric plug-in appliances wherever you need it. Special span-in plugs form part of the system. Take advantage of the accessibility of power to shorten leads on your equipment as trailing cables can cause accidents and perish quickly in any case. The system can be purchased in sets for fitting in existing kitchens as well as in component form for new installations.

MAKING EVERY INCH COUNT

Many people who complain that their kitchen is too small are not, in fact, short of space or lacking the means to use it properly. The reason is often that the room has been fitted with lots of standard units, with no thought given at the planning stage to where things will actually be stored.

It is not good enough to assume that most people's kitchens contain much the same selection of foods, utensils, kitchenwares, cleaning materials and so on and that therefore an experienced designer should be able to plan storage without consultation. No two people, let alone families, use their kitchens in quite the same way and it is therefore essential to make specific provision for everything you need to store.

The smaller the kitchen the more necessary is this detailed planning exercise. Go round your existing kitchen and make a list of everything that is in it plus everything else that you would like to include if you had the space. Then check this list against the layout plan you are considering. Write all over it if necessary – fresh copies are always easy to produce. Then present the designer with a list of left-overs for which you cannot see any obvious home.

On these pages are details of kitchens in which specific allowances have been made for particular requirements that are so often left to chance. Of course, changing needs have to be allowed for and there are obvious dangers in allowing just enough shelf space for the cookery books or spice jars you have collected so far. But if you have allocated some space for books and jars, you can at least choose how to use it. Far too many kitchens leave items like these out of the plan completely.

At first sight the kitchen on the right contains less storage space than the one above but in fact the only basic differences are the lack of a dishwasher and the choice of a smaller fridge. In this instance there is more serving and working space available, thanks in part to the use of an unusual slimline cooker.

Deeper worktops mean that some items are stored at the back and *also that the first shelf can be set lower. The plate rack, knife block and wall utensil rack are all practical space-savers. Old-fashioned sweet jars make excellent containers for sugar, flour and dried beans and pulses, and decorated tins of various sizes can be used to store anything from paper cake cups to packets of dried herbs and balls of string. There is so much room for per-* *sonal ingenuity in the detailing of this type of kitchen. Note how the bread board on the right doubles as a heat-proof surface for pans next to the cooker.*

PLANNING FOR EASY ACCESS

If you find your kitchen gets cluttered when you are working in it, you should blame not yourself, but the person who planned it. Far too many designers ignore the simple rule that if things are difficult to get at they are even more difficult to put away, especially when you are trying to do several things at once.

In an ideal world we would all have the time to collect the items we need before starting cooking and then to clear everything away before the cycle began again. The reality of most family kitchens is, of course, somewhat different.

When planning storage there are a few simple rules to follow. Make sure that everything you need regularly in a specific part of the kitchen can be reached without bending or stretching and without taking more than two steps to get at it. When planning where things are to go, ensure that the items you use most often are sited in the key zone of maximum access between hip and shoulder height; and remember that most people find it easier to walk an extra pace or so than to go down on hands and knees or to reach into the top of a high cupboard.

Next, plan the interiors of cupboards in such a way that everything in them can be reached without having to move something else first. Put small jars and bottles on the backs of doors or in baskets that can be pulled out. Use roll-out shelves or deep drawers to bring items out to you instead of reaching inside for them. Use removable containers which can be brought from a cupboard to your working area and then returned easily. Even simple ideas like using an old airtight cake tin for cake decorations can work well, so long as the tin itself can be reached reasonably easily.

Things to avoid, because they almost always mean bad access and waste of space, are deep, fixed shelves and the sort of design in which everything is packed away behind closed doors. Perhaps, if you are the sole user of your kitchen, and you have time both to hunt for things and to clear up as you go, an everything-hidden, showroom-style design can work for you, but for most people such designs are fit only for glossy furniture brochures.

In today's family kitchens, especially when space is at a premium, you cannot afford to be so wasteful of space and a certain amount of amiable clutter has to be accepted as part of the plan. The really tidy kitchen is not the one in which everything

disappears on special occasions, but in which it comes quite naturally to return everything to its place as you work, without making an effort or even thinking

Incidentally, by following this approach you can design kitchens for absolutely any special requirement. There really is nothing extra to consider, for example, when planning for someone who is physically disabled, blind or simply not as agile as they used to be. Just consider accessibility, and their range of movement, and everything will fall quite naturally into place. It is often suggested that special skills are required to design kitchens for the disabled, but you don't need to lack normal mobility in order to appreciate a room that makes cooking and other kitchen tasks less tiring and accident-prone.

In far too many kitchens the items you see here are jumbled together in a drawer or hidden away in a wall cupboard. By creating special fittings like these to make maximum use of the often-neglected midway area immediately above the worktop, makers like Bulthaup have solved the problem of where to store small, much-used items. The chopping board swings up when not required, hiding away the knife collection at the same time.

The same approach as that used by Bulthaup has been applied to the choice of cupboards throughout this entire kitchen. It would not be in the least difficult to find the perfect place to store everything, which means that every inch will be used and that wear and tear on both the kitchen and its users will be minimized.

LARDERS

The most important single element of storage in any kitchen is a really well-planned larder. It is often assumed that this cannot be the case in small rooms but in fact a larder that is properly planned can provide more accessible storage space in a given amount of floor area than any alternative arrangement.

The secret of a successful larder is planning the shelves and other fittings in such a way that every inch of potential space is used, yet all of the contents can be reached without having to move anything else. There are three possibilities: the traditional walk-in larder, which is part of the structure of the room; a big cupboard entirely fitted with pull-out basket drawers and roll-out shelves; and a double-door cupboard fitted with a variety of deep and shallow shelves, baskets, door-back racks and other specialized containers.

The second and third types are part of the range of alternative units offered by most makers of kitchen furniture but the walk-in larder will have to be made specifically to suit you and to fit the space available. It is the least expensive alternative but needs very careful thought. If you leave it to your carpenter to "put in a few shelves", these will almost certainly be too deep and set too far apart. So plan the whole of the interior in detail first, including door-back racks for bottles and small jars and removable baskets for vegetables and fruit. One really deep shelf at normal worktop height will be very useful, but most other shelves should probably be no more than 8–10 in. (200–250 mm) in depth.

The usefulness of your larder will be far greater if it is properly ventilated. On page 45 the ideal arrangement is illustrated, in which fresh air is piped into the larder at low level, leaves at high level and helps to ventilate the whole kitchen before leaving through the cooker hood or extractor. If your larder is sited on a cold wall, ensure that the inflow of air can be reduced or even cut off in really wintry weather so that vegetables and other contents are not frozen.

A marble or slate shelf makes an effective cooling slab but there is no point in fitting one unless your larder is properly ventilated. If it is, it will be the best place to set jellies, cool off cooked meat or other foods prior to freezing, store a small supply of wine and keep such things as fresh herbs, mature cheeses and exotic fruit in perfect condition.

Ventilating the larder from within the kitchen is not a satisfactory alternative, because most kitchens get too hot at least some of the time and stale cooking smells can be imparted to stored food. However, there is no need to go to great lengths to seal the doors of the larder so long as the ventilation system allows plenty of fresh air to enter freely from outside.

Try to position your larder somewhere in the kitchen where it will be equally accessible from both the main working area and the secondary area where others may be making snacks, tea or coffee. Ideally, set your fridge next to it for the same reason. Don't ever be tempted to keep the fridge or freezer in the larder itself, because they produce large amounts of hot air which would completely defeat the object of having a larder in the first place.

Don't confuse a larder with a specialized dry-goods store. Dry goods include not only packeted or dried foods but also tinned goods and those cookwares that do not need to be kept right next to the sink, cooker or pastry-making area for immediate and regular use. Although a dry-goods store may be constructed like a larder in many ways, it does not need to be ventilated with fresh air and can certainly house a fridge or freezer if you wish, because the heat produced will help to keep everything totally dry. Simply allow for sufficient air circulation to ensure that the cupboard does not actually become hot.

Finally make sure that every part of your larder can either be cleaned easily where it is or can be removed for cleaning. It is a very good idea, for instance, to line a walk-in larder completely with glazed tiles, although those on the floor should be non-slip. Storing items such as vegetables and fruit in lift-out plastic-covered wire baskets not only makes cleaning easier, but also enables you to take the entire container to your working area to sort out what is needed, which is much easier than doing the same job inside the store cupboard.

Left: It can be much cheaper to create a larder with partitioning and a house door than to buy a ready-made larder cupboard from a furniture manufacturer, though you will have to hunt for the fittings and plan the interior and ventilation carefully. Fit shallow-racks on the door back for small bottles, jars and packets; place a slab of stone at worktop height for cooling jellies and cooked meats. Ensure that the sizes and spacing of other shelves give you maximum access to the contents and arrange for through ventilation to keep everything fresh. Note the low level fresh air inlet with anti-frost shutter.

This ultimate fully-fitted larder by Bulthaup comes with a wide range of specially-shaped and fully-adjustable shelves, door baskets and lift-out trays to enable you to plan the interior to fit your own requirements and even vary the layout at different times of the year. The lowest shelf is metal covered and conceals the inlet point for cool air from outside. The door-controlled lighting unit above also contains an extractor fan which passes air from inside the cupboard out into the kitchen when the doors are closed. It has alternative settings for automatic and manual operation. You would need at least twice as much floor space to store the contents of this larder in any alternative type of cupboard, and it is unlikely that they would be as accessible as here.

BIG CUPBOARDS

It may seem a contradiction to say that the bigger the cupboard the more space it can save yet the secret of successful planning in many small kitchens is to concentrate most of the storage space in one or two really large cupboards, rather than trying to fit base and wall units all round the room. However, this will only be true if the space inside the large cupboards is used efficiently.

Some of the same rules that apply to planning a larder (see page 52) also apply to designing a big cupboard for chinaware, tinned and dried goods, pots and pans, cleaning equipment or indeed to house an entire laundry. In essence, ensure that everything in the cupboard can be reached without having to move something else first. There are a variety of ways in which this ideal can be attained. For instance, don't neglect to use the space on the back of the door for such things as racks of small jars or bottles, vacuum cleaner attachments or tins of polishes, spare cloths or rolls of kitchen paper.

Try to use shelves throughout which are only a little deeper than the items which are being stored on them and also avoid stacking items wherever possible. This applies particularly to chinaware. Stack plates no more than six high and reduce the vertical space between shelves to the minimum.

Really tall cupboards are often too deep to be really useful. They can be ideal places to store anything from chinaware to electrical gadgets (griddles, toasters, sandwich-makers and so on), but this is only true if everything is stored one item deep. It is far better to have a tall cupboard 1 ft (300 mm) deep containing 12 shelves than one 2 ft (600 mm) deep with only six. The true storage capacity of the two is potentially the same yet the first occupies half the floor space.

Large cupboards may also be devoted in part to housing built-in cookers or other appliances and in small kitchens it is absolutely vital to ensure that such equipment is fitted at the correct height, as bending in a confined space can be hazardous.

With really cheap kitchen furniture you usually have to take pot luck with the height at which built-in ovens or microwave cookers are inset. However, it is not usually difficult to alter heights to suit yourself and you may decide that spending a little more to get things right is a good investment.

The dimension which most people miscalculate is how high the top of a built-in oven should be. Assuming that your oven contains a grill, this should be placed so that the grill pan is about a

couple of inches (50 mm) below the eye height of the main user, so that you don't have to pull it out to see how things are cooking. In ovens where the grill compartment is above the main oven, once you have the grill in the correct position the chances are the oven below will be at a comfortable height.

It is almost always the case that when a cooker, fridge or freezer is built into a large cupboard, there is still some space left above, below or both, which is useful for storing associated items, such as baking trays, roasting tins or casseroles or spare airtight storage containers in the case of fridges or freezers. It used to be the case that a lot of space above and below built-in equipment was taken up with ventilation ducts but the latest cookers and fridges are much less demanding in this respect. Vertical dividers in a

cupboard space above an oven can be an excellent way to separate sets of oven trays, baking sheets and roasting tins, but in the space below built-in equipment it may well be worth considering the sort of pull-out storage discussed on pages 66–67.

Finally, consider creating a large cupboard to house laundering equipment or even a dishwasher. In the first case, whether you have chosen a combined washer-dryer or a separate washer and tumbler dryer which can be stacked, they can be hidden completely in a cupboard and the chances are there will still be some space for washing powders and perhaps even a laundry basket as well. In the case of a dishwasher, this can be floor standing or perhaps at waist level in the cupboard, with shelves for chinaware and pans in the rest of the space.

One of the best ways to use a corner is to create a larder or dry goods store in the space available. With some care in the planning of shelf spacings and the grouping of contents, it is often possible to pack a remarkable amount into a big cupboard which occupies very little actual floor area. This cupboard has a giant capacity, but because the door is set at an angle and the shelves inside are curved, you still have easy access to its contents. The bottom area is large enough to swallow two or three crates of beer and the shelves above are strong enough to cope with a month's supply of tinned pet food. The smaller the kitchen the more it can benefit from including a general-purpose store like this in the layout.

Left: The idea of a kitchen peppered with lots of shelves, wall racks, drawers of different sizes and specialized pull-out fittings may not appeal to you. Yet there is no doubt that if you want to use every inch of potential space but still be able to find things easily, whatever their shape and size, you do need a wide variety of different storage to suit individual items. In this big cupboard there are enough shelves, drawers and other types of racks and containers to ensure that all the contents are easy to get at, yet one door hides everything when access is not required.

Left: The storage capacity of this combined utility cupboard and dry goods store is considerable, yet it occupies little more than 6 sq. ft (0.6 sq. m) of floor space. There is no need to hunt through boxes or shelves for a particular tin of polish or cleaner fitting. Everything has its place. The use of roll-out shelves on the right means that you gain extra capacity by utilizing the "reaching space" that would be necessary between fixed shelves. Door-back racks and baskets ensure that even the smallest and most awkward items come right to hand when you need them.

SHELVES AND CUPBOARDS

In the early days of fitted kitchens the objective was to hide everything away behind closed doors when not in use but experience has shown that kitchens designed in this way give a completely false sense of organization. On the surface everything may look orderly but you will probably need second sight to find many items, even those in regular use.

Perhaps in the days when the kitchen was used by only one person and that person was a full-time housewife, the "all behind doors" style worked adequately enough. But today's kitchens are generally family rooms. It must be easy for anyone to find foods, utensils and cookwares and just as easy for them to clear up as they go along.

The more accessible things are the better, especially in a small kitchen where several people may be doing different things at the same time. To be accessible, everything should be visible, and as something stored in a cupboard cannot be immediately visible even if you know which cupboard it is in, it might be argued that the perfect kitchen would have nothing stored behind cupboard doors.

Why have cupboards in a kitchen anyway?

The first answer most people will think of is "to keep things tidy" but is that really the case? The sort of tidiness they are referring to is probably that superficial sense of order which quickly breaks down when you look behind the doors. That approach only works if you spend time tidying away and looking for things that are hidden when you are working, so where is the real saving in labour?

A more valid reason is "to keep things clean", yet even in this case it is worth asking why your kitchen should be such a dirty place in which to store things. Is everything hidden away behind doors in your living room and dining room? Of course not. So why accept that the place where you prepare food should not be as naturally clean and hygienic as your living room? In fact the only reason why most kitchens are dirtier than they should be is that they are not properly ventilated, and surely it is better to solve that problem and as a result create a truly labour-saving area?

In a properly ventilated, naturally clean kitchen far more of the things in regular use can be kept out in the open where they are always on view and therefore totally accessible. If you feel that your kitchenwares, storage jars, china and pans are not attractive enough to be on view, it will cost less to

Left: In one of their latest designs, Bosch show that visibility at least need not be a problem with enclosed storage. Note that they have also found some bonus storage space on the front of a compact extractor canopy above the cooker.

Right: Innovators Bulthaup offer adjustable shelving in two depths on a matching back panel. To the left is yet another kind of storage, a wall cupboard fitted with a vertical roller shutter door. The idea is that you open this when you start work, use it just like an open shelf unit and roll down the shutter again when you have finished. To the left of the sink, the small cutting board in front of the inset knife block can be lifted out to gain access to a waste bin below.

replace them than to buy cupboards in which to hide them away.

There are of course good reasons why every kitchen needs some cupboards. The larders that we looked at on the previous page are one example and the space below the sink for a waste bin, bucket and cloths, washing-up liquid reserve and bottle of bleach is another. Apart from these cases, always think carefully before putting a cupboard door between you and what you are storing.

If you share the kitchen with young children, cupboard doors become a necessity rather than a choice. Pets can also be a good reason to opt for doors, as even the best ventilation system cannot deal with dog and cat hairs.

Yet despite all of these practical points there is a very good case for storing far more on open shelves than has been common practice in the past few years, especially above worktop height. Many

furniture makers have appreciated the advantages of this approach and a wide range of alternatives is available.

If you are fitting the kitchen yourself, consider one of the adjustable wall-strip systems that are now available, where changes can be made from time to time to suit new requirements. One advantage of "doing it yourself" is that you can consider a third alternative to open or closed storage and that is fitting roller blinds which pull down in front of the open shelves when the kitchen is not in use. If the kitchen area is in one corner of a larger, multi-purpose room, this simple idea allows you to have the best of both worlds – totally accessible storage which simply disappears when you sit down to eat or relax.

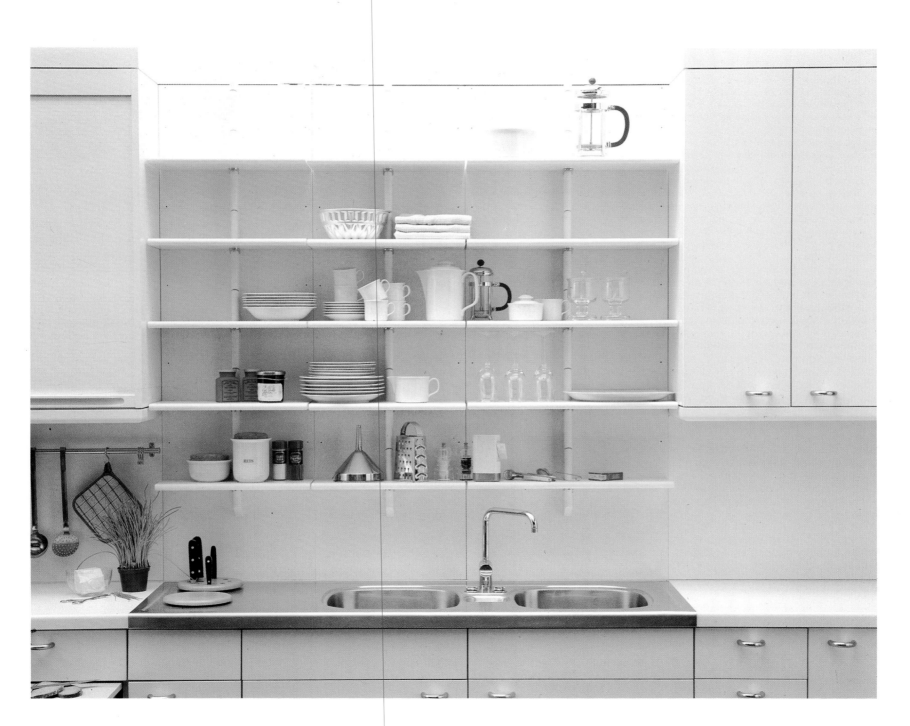

DRAWERS

Cabinet and unit drawers are useful because they provide a method of storing a variety of kitchen items out of sight until needed. However, to take full advantage of this type of storage, you must ensure that the drawers you choose are the right size and that specific compartments are created for small items. It is no good having two or three drawers allocated to cutlery or small utensils if you have to search through all of them every time you want a potato peeler or a small vegetable knife.

Cutlery dividers, whether created as part of a drawer or as drop-in containers, are useful for far more than table cutlery. Most drawers are deeper than they need to be for storing small items, so two-layer dividers can double your storage space. Use the lower tray for those items which you are likely to need less often.

Deep pan drawers, usually with removable plastic-covered wire surrounds, are now offered by most furniture suppliers. You may find that to get maximum use out of these, pans have to be stacked within the drawer. This not only reduces accessibility but in the case of non-stick pans can give rise to damage, so try to store your pans in drawers which provide the depth you require and no more. In fact it is better to find somewhere in the kitchen where small and shallow pans can be hung up or stored on a shallow shelf rather than in a special pan drawer.

The same approach applies to smaller items. Find odd corners in which you can fit some really small box drawers for balls of string, pencils and thumb tacks, not to mention all the other small impedimenta which usually inhabit drawers or cupboards that are better suited to larger things.

Longer box drawers, which can either be pulled out partly or taken right to the surface where you are working are very useful for grouping things together. Divide one for different types of dried beans, another for a range of pastas and a third for cake decorations and tart cups. A fourth could be used for patisserie tools and a fifth for rolls of foil, plastic bags and greaseproof paper.

Think about where you are going to keep your kitchen tool set: a hammer, a couple of screwdrivers, pliers, wire cutters and either fuses or fuse wire. By far the best place is in a drawer at plinth level, which can also be useful for storing such things as spare roasting tins and bakeware that you only use on special occasions.

Drawers can also be used successfully to store items that are usually kept on shelves. Tinned goods, for instance, can be kept on their sides in a drawer, so long as it is designed to take the weight. Most packets of dry foods are labelled on the top as well as the side, so drawer storage can be totally practical for dried fruits, flour, sugar and many other pre-packed ingredients.

Drawers are also suitable for storing herbs and spices which are best protected from light. The drawer should be divided into small sections and fitted with an inner lid of Perspex, so that you can label each compartment with its contents. Many items, such as bay leaves and nutmegs, can be kept loose but make the sections just large enough to take the spice jars.

It is better not to keep sharp knives in a drawer, but if you do, try to obtain a suitable flat block which will ensure that every knife has its place, where it will be kept apart from others and you can reach it without risk of cutting yourself.

Specialized containers which can be fitted in cupboards, for storing bread, vegetables, spices and other items form another category of drawer. As in the case of baskets in a larder, these enable you to create specific homes for groups of items that are best stored together. Several furniture makers offer special bread storage fittings which include a board and somewhere to keep the knife.

A number of traditional ideas are now being revived to meet special storage requirements as well. Butlers' trays, which can be pulled out like a drawer or taken right out to a working position, are excellent for storing dried ingredients, table silver, sets of cloths and napkins, really fragile chinaware (if the tray is fitted with tailored divisions) and sets of special utensils. For instance, you might have an "Indian cookery" tray containing the relevant utensils, spices and dried ingredients. We generally store like with like in the kitchen but there is a case to be made for keeping some things together which are almost always used with each other.

Above: Cutlery is best kept in shallow divided trays, so why not fit two trays in one normal-depth drawer? One of many storage ideas which are the essence of the latest designs from German furniture-makers SieMatic.

Below: Where better to hide a set of folding steps than in the otherwise wasted plinth space below a base cupboard? Many manufacturers offer this handy accessory. This example is by Bulthaup. Kitchen tools might be kept there too.

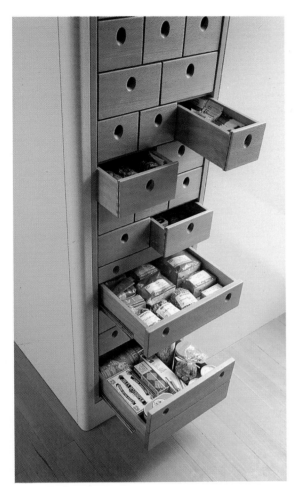

Above: old apothecary drawers were the inspiration for this unusual store for spices and other small items. The smaller box drawers above can be pulled right out and taken to where you are working, which makes them ideal for cake decorations, sets of special utensils or other items often used together.

Right: Another of the apothecary drawer ideas, this time in a more rustic style. The total amount of storage space is immense, but without some form of labelling you are likely to need great patience, an exceptional memory or the instincts of a veteran explorer to find what you are seeking.

WALL AND MIDWAY STORAGE

The least useful, yet most commonplace, approach to storing things above worktop height is to fit closed cupboards with fixed shelves. Yet most of the items we store at that height are relatively small – jars, packets, tins and chinaware. Almost all these can be stored more space-efficiently and accessibly in other places, such as a larder, drawer or tall shallow china cupboard, but the most important point is that normal wall cupboards leave the vital 'midway' area above the worktop completely unused.

No matter what size your kitchen is, if you do not use this space for storage or utensils you are making work for yourself. All the items you could store there will be less accessible wherever else you choose to put them.

As a result, most kitchen designers and furniture makers now go to great lengths to make full use of this zone of maximum accessibility. Racks are provided for utensils and spice jars, specially-fitted small cupboards for plug-in gadgets, even small baskets for fruit and carriers for chopping boards.

The depth of working surfaces tends to be standardized around the sizes of major built-in appliances but most people need deeper tops. In practice we only use the front half of a working surface for working on and the back half contains the

equipment and ingredients we happen to be using at the time. To some extent, storing things on the wall immediately behind the worktop can reduce the value of that back area, so making the top about 4 in. (100 mm) deeper has much to recommend it. In a cooking and serving area it means you have more space for plates around the hob, and in the food preparation area it means you can keep utensils and other things up on the wall without reducing your effective working area.

The Italian company Arclinea created a whole new concept around this idea of using the midway area as effectively as possible by extending it upwards to the maximum height that can be reached in comfort without stretching and then fitting short closed cupboards above. By varying the depth of racks and shelves in this larger midway area to fit the arc through which the arm swings naturally, they considerably increased the volume of truly accessible storage immediately around the main working zone, while keeping the secondary long-term storage area above dust-free.

At about the same time the German manufacturers Bulthaup introduced another solution to the same problem. They offered two types of wall cupboard, both fitted with roller-shutter blinds which open to leave the shelves within completely accessi-

ble. The smaller cupboards replace normal wall units, but offer many of the advantages of open shelves. The larger cupboards extend right down to the worktop, offering both a means of covering in what would otherwise be exposed midway storage and also an elegant way of shutting away such things as food mixers and processors when these are not in use.

Many ways of hiding food mixers and processors have been developed over the years but most have either involved special spring-loaded cupboard fittings which are prone to failure in time or made the machine less accessible. Bulthaup's idea of "worktop wall cupboards" with big roller-shutters and specially-designed internal racks for accessories is the best to come forward so far and the model has been widely copied.

Poggenpohl tackled the requirement in a different way, leaving the depth of their worktops at the standard 24 in. (600 mm), but creating midway units designed to extend further back behind this line. Theoretically, this leads to a waste of space behind the base cupboards and the wall cupboards above, but when that space is used to run service pipes below or to set a small oven flush with the line of the wall cupboard fronts, the potentially accessible space lost may well be negligible.

Poggenpohl's "System 75" shifts the normal worktop forward 6 in. (150 mm) so that the total distance from the front edge to the wall is increased to 30 in. (750 mm). The actual worktop can then be either the normal depth of 24 in. (600 mm), in which case some items can be stored in the gap created at the rear, or the full 30 in. (750 mm) deep, allowing space for *appliances at the back without reducing the effective work surface in front. Some special extra-deep storage units have already been developed to take advantage of the potential storage beneath these extended tops, and the system also offers interesting possibilities for the siting of hidden radiators, hot water tanks and other equipment in the bonus space which it creates.*

Worktop wall cupboards fitted with vertical roller shutter doors have solved some of the most difficult kitchen storage problems. The base of the cupboard is the worktop itself, so that a food processor or coffee maker can simply be pushed back into the cupboard (still plugged in) and the shutter pulled down when you have finally finished work. With the shutter up, you don't have to keep opening a door to get at the contents. Different internal fittings and adjustable shelf positions enable you to adapt such cupboards to a range of storage needs.

Many traditional kitchen ideas still work well. Here Tielsa show an interesting version of the glazed dresser. Placing the small box drawers in the base has two advantages. They are ideal for storing small items and also ensure that the doors above can be opened without having to clear the surface in front first.

CORNER STORAGE

Corners in small kitchens are more than just places where two walls happen to meet. They are potentially valuable storage areas which can be equally accessible from either side. Corners may also be used as key working areas, centred on a hob or sink (see pages 24 and 40).

There is an argument for simply blocking off corners below worktop height and ignoring them if there are worktops on both sides because then the space on each side of the corner can be used for anything you like. Any sort of cupboard that reaches round into the corner area reduces the storage effectively available immediately behind the door.

However, few people will adopt such a technical view and most will opt for one of the alternatives. The conventional solution is to use a carousel unit of some sort, either just from one side or going right the way round. As carousels are prone to damage in time if heavily loaded, ensure that you select a sturdily-built model. Alternatively fit a diagonal cupboard directly into the corner, which may simply be shelved for the long-term storage of bulky items or fitted entirely with deep drawers. Some furniture makers create a feature with these corner cupboards, providing them with curved doors below curved corner worktops. However, virtually any type

of base cupboard can be used satisfactorily within its inherent limitations.

At wall level the problem is greater because it is very difficult to reach into orthodox corner wall units. It is a better idea to have open shelves in the corner and probably best of all to sacrifice a little potential space, fit a false wall across the corner and have shelves of normal depth set at an angle. The space behind can often be used to hide runs of central heating pipes or a soil drain from a bathroom above.

Perhaps the best use of a corner area is as a site for a larder. This gives you access to the whole of the potential space available but means you can use quite a small door to reach it. In such an arrangement it is often most efficient to place your fridge and freezer in tall cabinets next to the larder, a dry-goods store next to them and so on, so that all your main storage is concentrated in one compact area.

These large corner cabinets are very awkward to handle once they have been assembled, so do ensure that either you assemble them in the kitchen itself before installing them or that your doors are large enough for a ready-made cupboard to pass through.

One of the best ways to exploit potential corner storage space is with a full carousel. However, some are either not very strongly made or involve tricky catches or centring devices. This model by Spanish furniture makers Xey is robust and easy to use. The curved door and worktop are typical features of many modern styles now offered by leading manufacturers. While not forgetting the essentially functional role of their products, kitchen furniture-makers are following a trend towards softer lines and away from bland utilitarian units.

This striking yet totally practical corner sink is made by Villeroy & Boch in Asterite. It is designed to be inset flush into working surfaces of laminated plastic or other materials. Accessories include the small secondary bowl seen on the left which converts the main sink into a preparation zone. A drop-in colander of the same size is also available. The advantages of a corner sink are that it enables you to make good use of space which might otherwise be wasted and leaves room clear for working or serving on both sides.

COOKS' KITCHENS

There are probably now more people who cook for pleasure as much as for necessity than ever before and the range of ingredients available is almost endless. This means that kitchens are increasingly designed not only as functional family rooms which are attractive to work in, but also as specialized workshops with storage, equipment and surfaces planned around the practical needs of the cookery enthusiast.

This growth of interest in specialized and international cookery has created new problems for kitchen designers. Ingredients and methods of preparation and cooking vary from one part of the world to the other, and this is reflected in different storage requirements and the types of equipment and utensils used. Eastern cookery, for example, calls for many special ingredients. You may need to stock up to 40 herbs and spices in all and many special dried and preserved foods, some of which are quite bulky. Practically every type of Eastern cookery calls for special pans if the authentic flavours and textures are to be accurately recreated. These not only have to be stored somewhere when not in use but can pose other problems as they may not work satisfactorily on normal European or American cooking equipment.

The most common requirement is storage for a full set of traditional cook's knives and the chopping and carving boards essential in their use. The simplest solution is to use hardwood worktops, probably maple, plus a portable knife block. However, a normal knife block cannot cope with really large knives and boards still have to be used for most cutting.

Drop-down cutting blocks, which hinge up against the wall when not in use, are now offered by many furniture-makers. Sometimes these are arranged so that when you drop the board your set of knives comes into view. In other cases smaller boards, which are easier to take to the sink for cleaning, are hung on the wall in sets and knives may be stored in a block set into the worktop.

If you spend much time at the cooking hob, try to arrange for it to be set at a lower height than your main worktop. This not only makes handling large pans easier but you can see into pans more easily as well. You may also find that an unorthodox hob arrangement is helpful; for example, one which places pans in a row instead of two behind two, so that you do not have to reach over one to get to another.

Hanging racks come into their own in the cook's kitchen. They provide the best possible way to ensure that the utensils and pans you use most are always readily to hand. Try to make provision for a rack to hold recipes away from the worktop. Some furniture-makers offer recipe holders which hinge down from below wall cupboards.

A large marble or granite surface should be included in your design if you do much pastry-making by hand rather than machine. Make sure you choose a stone which does not stain or scratch, such as those recommended on page 70, or have the entire surface made up for you in Corian, a solid plastic which will outlast normal plastic laminates by many years.

Solid hardwood tops are probably the first choice for keen cooks. They are naturally non-slip and less likely to suffer major damage from sharp knives or hot pans. It is worth considering setting blocks of suitable marble or granite or even sheets of stainless steel into the wood surface at points where you require exceptional resistance to wear or heat, but well-made tops of maple or iroko will give a lifetime of excellent service with a minimum of attention.

Your plans will need to take account of the necessity to store a growing collection of cookery books and somewhere to read them in comfort. If you are prone to back trouble, you may well appreciate the special "standing stool" created by Alno which gives excellent support but is easy to move around the kitchen.

As you probably have to store a considerable number of specialized gadgets and utensils, consider an entire cupboard made up of small drawers and boxes. Perhaps the best example is that offered by Bulthaup. This unit can be ordered with the proportion of large drawers to small pull-out boxes that suits your own requirements and its ability to give you instant access to lots of specialized items is unique.

Many specialized forms of cookery call for special equipment. The Chinese wok is probably the best example, even though very few domestic hobs are capable of heating a traditional wok satisfactorily. Jenn-Air produce an electrically-heated wok element for their modular hob system and the latest halogen ring ceramic hobs are certainly better than orthodox electric hotplates. However, in practice, one of the two-ring gas hobs with a large main burner works most effectively.

Other major makers of cooking equipment have produced many items to meet special requirements such as these: Gaggenau's pizza brick in their 700-series ovens; Imperial's built-in pressure-cooker/steamer; Atag's multiple kebab skewer fittings for their hot-air ovens. Many of these extra pieces of cooking equipment are in fact adaptations of basic ovens and hobs, so they take up no additional space and are as available to those with small kitchens as they are to others. It is possible to build up specialized cooking areas by using combinations of modular hob units, but in a small kitchen it is usually easier to gain this extra capacity by installing a large-capacity microwave cooker, such as the Sharp 8120 or 8320, which offers a hot-air cooking facility as well.

It is the choice of main oven however that is likely to be most influenced by specialized cookery requirements. The latest generation of ovens are discussed on pages 18–19, but if you want an oven with special capabilities, such as bottom heat only for traditional French casseroling or identical temperatures at all levels for batch baking, the latest multi-function ovens offer such features combined with a compactness and operating economy which would certainly have been considered unattainable ten years ago.

Many manufacturers now offer specialized fittings to those who demand proper surfaces for working on and racks for knives and utensils. These are part of the Bosch range. The cutting block swings up to cover the knife rack when the worktop is required for other purposes.

In this tiny cooking zone, also by Bosch, all the rules of good layout have still been followed. There is ample space each side of the hob for working and serving and the utensils, flavourings, spices and other materials often required in cookery are near at hand.

PULL-OUT STORAGE

One of the best ways of maximizing the use of space in your kitchen is to use cupboard interior fittings which pull right out on runners when you wish to get at the contents. Although they cost more than simple cupboards with shelves, pull-out interiors enable you to store twice as much in the same space because you do not need to waste an inch in allowing for access.

Even if you have room for extra cupboards, pull-out storage is more economical so long as you choose the right fittings. Simply asking for a range of pull-out baskets and roll-out shelves is not the answer because you will only gain extra storage if the fittings are specifically suited to what you will be storing in them.

Fitting roll-out shelves in a base cupboard should enable you to have three movable shelves where there would have been space for only two that were fixed. The reason is that with a roll-out shelf you can do away with reaching space. The same is true with the roll-out larder interiors which are now offered by so many makers. These are usually designed to allow you to change the position of the baskets or shelves on the carrier frame, so you can pack them as tight as access to their contents will allow. Only then will you be able to fit more storage baskets and therefore gain the maximum use of the floor-space involved. As a bonus, you will be able to get at the contents much more easily as well.

The key to this approach is checking the planned contents of your new kitchen against the layout plan, as suggested on page 48. Once you know what you want to store in a given position you can then select the interior fitting which is most appropriate.

Below sinks, for instance, consider fitting a complete roll-out base just above the bottom of the cupboard, divided into sections for cleaning materials, bottles of bleach and detergent, a bucket, spare cleaning cloths and so on. This makes it much easier and safer to get at all the bits and pieces which tend to accumulate under the sink. But it is a good idea to mount your waste bin or bins separately, to save pulling out the whole lot every time you want to throw something away.

Pull-out drawers also make pan storage much easier, though there is a temptation to stack saucepans and casseroles if the drawer is too deep. Consider instead a multi-level pull-out basket arrangement, with a place for every pan and a shallow tray for lids at the top. These are now available as accessories to fit almost any type and size of cupboard.

There are various different fittings available for storing bottles in a cupboard, ranging from trays that carry an entire crate of beer to racks for cooking wine, oils and mixers. Another type of useful pull-out is a towel rail, though it should be fitted in a position where air can circulate freely around it.

Alternatively, you can buy a pull-out rail set fitted with an electrical air heater.

Though not strictly a pull-out arrangement but achieving similar accessibility, carousel racks are now being offered by some companies as interior fittings in tall larder or dry goods cupboards. Whereas access to the contents of shelves in a conventional carousel in a corner base cupboard is still somewhat limited, these larder arrangements have the advantage that everything they contain is presented at a convenient height.

In most cases such new cupboards are designed specifically to be fitted into a corner, where the potential disadvantage of wasted angles which applies to all carousels is less of a problem.

One very useful type of pull-out storage which is now becoming increasingly popular is the box drawer. Box drawers are rather like traditional apothecary drawers in that they can if you wish be taken out of the cupboard to the place in the kitchen where you are working. This makes them particularly useful for groups of small items which tend to be used together. Good examples are sets of special cake decorating utensils and materials, of paper cake-cups or cake candles and holders.

If you turn to pages 154 to 161, which examine the planning of specific working areas in the kitchen, you will see that we have allowed for pull-out storage in several cases. It is worth checking your own requirements against these ideas.

Some makers create entire units which pull out in the form of trolleys, such as this beer crate truck and bottle carrier by Bosch. Another Bosch idea is to have one of their Gourmet 2000 series combined microwave/oven/grills built into a trolley which fits below a worktop and also contains space for microwave cookware and other accessories. The oven can therefore be used where it stands in the kitchen or rolled out to the dining area or even to another room for snack-making or finishing off a meal at the table.

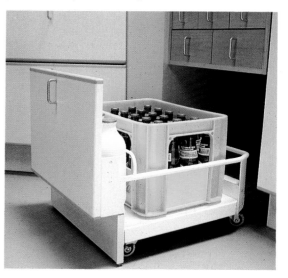

A wide variety of pull-out foodstores is now available on the market and many of them offer different sizes and types of basket fittings to enable you to design the interior to meet your personal requirements. In this version the pull-out section has been split in two. This is a sensible idea because otherwise it is easy to overload the runner system. Note that pull-out storage has also been selected below the built-in oven. It is an excellent choice when you have to find space for lots of roasting tins, baking trays and sheets and a couple of big casseroles.

KITCHEN TABLES

Traditionally, the table is the centre of all kitchen activity. In old kitchens it was the most important multi-purpose working surface in the room and also acted as the gathering-point for the family at mealtimes.

Today relatively few kitchens are large enough to contain a central table but whenever possible some provision should be made for a second level of working surface and a place where light meals can be taken. A good deal of ingenuity is used by furniture-makers to overcome this problem.

One possibility is to have a pull-out table which is hidden inside a cupboard when not in use. This can be an excellent solution in cases where the table will only be used for meals or perhaps to assemble courses of a major meal to be eaten elsewhere in the house. At most times it can be away out of sight and the space it would occupy is available for working in.

Other ways to achieve the same effect are to have a folding table which stands in a corner or even hangs on the wall when not in use or a flap which hinges either up or down onto the wall. The thing to remember with pull-out or fold-away tables is that unless they are well-made and robust it may not be long before they become unstable and therefore impractical to use.

It can be argued that the modern equivalent to the old kitchen table is the peninsula or even the breakfast bar. Peninsulas are useful to provide a natural break between the working and eating or visiting areas in a kitchen but some thought has to be given to the height of the peninsula surface.

It is more comfortable to eat at normal table height, which is approximately 30 in. (750 mm), than at what is now regarded as standard worktop height – 36 in. (900 mm). But on the other hand you need more space to withdraw a chair from a table and step away from it than you do if you sit at a high surface on a stool. Also, for a peninsula working surface to be of much value it needs to be at least 24 in. (600 mm) wide. A breakfast bar set at a different level to this, perhaps at table height, needs to be about 16 in. (400 mm) wide to be comfortable to eat at.

Alternatively, if you create a peninsula with the working and eating sections at the same level, it can be as little as 36 in. (900 mm) wide and will work very well. The decision then lies between setting the whole surface at table height or normal main worktop height and if space is really restricted the choice will probably be for normal worktop height, using stools for seating, which require less circulation space and can be completely hidden below the surface when not in use.

Narrower peninsulas are only workable if they are open below though you can certainly fit shallow drawers under the working surface without creating a cramped space. Do not even consider setting a cooking hob or sink in such a narrow peninsula. The hob would be downright dangerous, as pans would be too easy to reach from the eating side, often occupied by children; and the sink would result in water splashing onto the floor. However, hobs or sinks in peninsulas that are 36 in. (900 mm) or more wide can work very well indeed.

The latest idea on kitchen tables is for short peninsulas, probably projecting no more than 30 in. (750 mm) at most from the line of the base cupboards and generally made of solid maple or beech, so that they can be used as food preparation areas. These can also double up as domestic snack bars, though they are hardly adequate for family meals. However, they can solve the requirement for a second lower working surface in the kitchen, to be used for pastry-making and food-processing. It is also an ideal height for hob cooking.

The fact that it is safer and less tiring to cook at a somewhat lower level than that which is ideal for the sink has been known for centuries, though the knowledge appears to have been lost in the 1920s and rediscovered along with the new science of kitchen ergonomics in the 1950s. Traditional kitchen ranges were always made between 32 in. (800 mm) and 34 in. (850 mm) high. Many solid fuel stoves are still made to this standard, though many installers have forgotten why and set them on plinths so that they align with the main worktops.

The wish of manufacturers to standardize everything is probably the main reason why most kitchens contain only one working surface height, but it is a poor excuse. The way to arrive at the ideal working heights for your kitchen is explained on page 158, but if you are incorporating the equivalent of a kitchen table in your new plan, it is well worth considering setting it at the lower height and using it as a combined cooking, food-processing, meal assembly and eating area.

Pull-out tables like this can be used to increase the working surfaces in kitchens that are too small to allow more permanent tops to be fitted. Such a pull-out table may be used for extra food preparation, perhaps for a major family gathering or dinner party, or when the time comes to assemble the meal before taking it through to the dining room. This particular table is strongly constructed and when not in use curls up into the space normally occupied by a drawer.

This strongly constructed, cantilevered working surface is a permanent fixture but the fact that no supports are necessary means that it does not form a visual block in a small room. It is large enough for two people to use, one working at the hob to the left and the other at the oven to the right. There is enough unobstructed leg space below for people to eat a light meal, sitting on tall stools on both sides. Note the lacquered metal storage rack hanging above, very much a Bulthaup design trademark.

WORKTOPS

The most common working surface for kitchens is laminated plastic. It is relatively cheap, easy to shape, bend, cut and install, but has the great disadvantage that it cannot be repaired if damaged. It is hardly surprising therefore that many alternatives are now available which, though they are all more expensive, have other advantages to offer. The most promising of these is a new type of plastic laminate which is the same colour right through. It still shows scratch marks but normal wear and tear takes much longer to make the surface unsightly.

It has become commonplace to use tiles for working surfaces, though they need expert fitting with specialized materials to be completely satisfactory. Shiny tiles should be avoided because they probably contain poisonous metals in the glaze, and you should ensure that the tiles you plan to use are tough enough not to crack. Even so, keep a few spares in case of accidents. Opinions vary on how hygienic tiled tops are in practice and it is certainly true that you will need to use boards and slabs for most food preparation.

Corian is a solid plastic material which has some of the visual character of marble but can be worked with sharp hand tools. It can also be used to create completely seamless worktops of any shape or size, together with curved edges and upstands and even moulded-in sinks. It is extremely expensive however – much more so than granite, for example, and it does not have the everlasting qualities of real stone.

Stone is now used quite often for kitchen worktops but it should be selected with great care. Virtually all types of marble, for instance, are unsuitable for general use because the polished surface will quickly be destroyed by fresh citrus fruit juices. All marbles stain easily with blood, fish juices and many other common food ingredients, although on dark patterned marbles the marks may not be easily visible.

Granite is probably the ideal working stone, though you should be careful in your selection. Some granites are prone to cracking due to natural faults in the rock and others have a porous structure, so that, while they may not stain, liquids are absorbed, which causes a colour change and is clearly unhygienic.

Probably the best worktop granite is Cornish Grey. It is very hard, reasonably proof against cracking and impossible to damage in normal use. Unlike darker stones, it rarely reflects dazzle from

lights, and it is the easiest surface available to keep in perfect condition.

There are several other suitable greys, many of which are not as visually severe as Cornish Grey. But if you want something prettier, opt for Pink Porrino, which is very similar in character, though some types are porous, so be careful to check with your supplier. There are a number of attractive and practical brown granites, and if you want something really spectacular opt for black. Most black granites make excellent worktops but they need a lot of cleaning and you must plan your lighting carefully to avoid irritating glare and reflections.

Solid hardwoods, mainly maple and beech, are now becoming commonplace in the best kitchens. They make very "friendly" surfaces which need little care other than an occasional oiling and will probably look better after 20 years than they did the day they were installed. Elm and oak are recommended, though oak must not be allowed to absorb water as it blackens. Iroko and teak are both excellent, though teak is now very expensive. Sycamore is similar to maple, though not as hard. It is a lighter wood and retains its lightness, whereas most woods darken in time. Softwoods should be avoided, even if varnished, because they tend to splinter.

Generally it is best not to attempt to seal hardwood worktops. But they should be oiled regularly with nothing more specialized than clean corn or groundnut oil which will effectively seal the surface against most potential stains. Between times wash the worktop as you would a plastic surface and remove any unsightly scratches either with wire wool or, if they are deep, a cabinet scraper.

Don't be tempted to use "end grain" maple tops because unless they are kept moist shrinkage will cause severe cracking. It is better to have a small portable block for chopping which can be taken to the sink for cleaning. Iroko and sycamore are the best woods for chopping boards made to fit into sinks for vegetable preparation, though sycamore is a little prone to twisting.

If you are considering inset working slabs rather than entire worktops, marble is a good choice. White marble is a classic for pastry slabs (and cooling slabs in larders) because it tends to reflect heat, but many people prefer to make pastry on wood, particularly beech and ash. Maple is almost certainly the best choice for cutting boards as it is practically impossible to produce splinters in normal use even over many years.

Try to make space for several boards of different sizes, so that you can reserve some for special purposes. It is a good idea to keep one just for meat, and the best material is probably one of the approved commercial plastics, such as Rowplas or Solidur, as these can be kept clean to a standard which is impossible with any other material except perhaps stainless steel.

Once regarded as the ultimate working surface material for keen cooks and still ideal if you are concerned with total hygiene (perhaps because someone in your family suffers from a food allergy), stainless steel is not the friendliest surface to work on and can ruin the best kitchen knives all too easily. However, there is a case to be made for setting pieces of stainless steel flush into the surface of wood tops where there may be a risk of severe wear or perhaps scorching.

For most people however, the first choice is still likely to be plastic laminate, mainly because of availability and low cost. It is worth remembering that fitting solid wood front edges to laminate tops and ensuring that joins between sheets are all well away from areas where there is often water about will probably extend their working life in good condition for many years. Also, try to ensure that there are always lots of boards to hand for hot pans, preparing vegetables and slicing bread.

When planning worktops for a small kitchen it is best to consider each working area in turn, choosing the most appropriate surface for each situation. It is important to remember that in small kitchens worktops inevitably get tougher use than they do in large rooms where work is spread over a greater area. Therefore a good choice would be a Corian top with moulded-in double sink for the dishwashing zone, a maple top for the food preparation area and either a granite or marble slab for pastry-making which doubles as a heat-proof surface next to the oven or hob.

Top left: Worktops of wood are now exceptionally popular, partly because they age gracefully compared with the plastic alternatives. Some woods, such as maple, sycamore and iroko, need no special treatment other than occasional oiling, but the pine top shown here will have to be resealed with a hard clear lacquer from time to time to protect it from both abrasion and water.

Left: Corian has all the advantages of plastic laminates but, as it is a solid material, it is far more resistant to wear and tear over the years. It can be joined seamlessly into continuous tops, and twin sinks like these can be moulded in, with grooved draining areas formed to one side or the other if you wish. Visually, it has some of the properties of marble and it remains cool to the touch in almost every situation.

Above right: Increasingly popular, granite tops share with stainless steel the advantage of being proof against virtually any sort of abuse and accidental damage. Not all types of granite are equally suitable, however, so you should check the properties of the sort you are considering with a specialist. Here the stone top has been fitted with wood edging, which introduces a softer feeling to the design than that given by an all-stone top.

As kitchens are now often regarded as living areas as well as workshops, you might think that planning the decor would simply be a matter of applying all the rules which are well established for other areas of the house. With large kitchens there is probably some truth in this because you have the space in which to make ideal choices about where things will be placed, how they will be lit and how areas of colour and texture will be related. In a small kitchen you probably do not have that luxury and there is a real risk that by the time you have solved all the practical problems of getting the best use out of the space available, you may end up with a jumble of conflicting colours, shapes and relationships which is practically impossible to resolve.

With small kitchens, there has to be a planned approach to the use of colour, the choice of materials for furniture and worktops and for all the accessories, storage jars and other items which contribute to the final appearance and atmosphere of the room. As with so many aspects of kitchen design, you will find that you have to compromise right away and this is especially true with small kitchens.

Aspects that you will not be able to control include the proportions of the room, which may be unsatisfactory, and awkward but unalterable features, such as windows which are too large or too small. Sometimes you can turn an odd shape or angle into a positive feature, even though at first it might prevent you from doing something you want to do. You may be able to hide your problem feature by building over it or incorporating it within a piece of furniture. If not, you have two options: either make it disappear by painting it the same colour as the background tone you choose for the room or emphasize the discord by painting it a bright, contrasting colour. Examples of both these solutions can be found on pages 80 and 98.

Sometimes you cannot avoid re-using old equipment in a new kitchen or buying machines from different makers which may be visually incompatible. One solution is to have the items resprayed, just as you would a car. This does not work satisfactorily with cookers or hobs, unless they are completely stripped down and re-enamelled by a specialist, but any car accident repair workshop can put a sparkling new face on your old fridge, washing machine, dryer or dishwasher.

The utensils and accessories that are part of the working decor of any kitchen come in many colours, shapes and sizes. You may be prepared to replace many of them when you refit the kitchen so that they blend in with your new colour scheme, but it is worth keeping in mind that future additions may not be so easy to match as fashions in accessory colours change. One answer to this problem is to ensure that your appliances and utensils are invisible when they're not in use.

The same goes for cooking ingredients and manufacturer's packages. Unless everything is going to be locked away behind doors, these will become part of the kitchen decor and an element over which you will have little control as time passes. Similarly, you cannot ensure that all your cookery books match, and although telephones are available in a wide range of colours, TV sets and radios are not. These factors need to be considered because the temptation when dealing with a small kitchen is to use a simple, low-key approach to decor, either making everything possible white on the assumption that this will make the room look larger or by concentrating on neutral beiges and light wood finishes.

The snag with both white and pale neutral colours is that they show minor marks too readily and tend to age quickly. In any case, the all-white approach is often counter-productive because the eye is automatically drawn even to quite small areas of colour, and unless these are very carefully controlled the kitchen may appear to be visually cluttered even when it is not.

It is far better in practice to decide on certain features in the kitchen, either existing or created, and emphasize them visually to draw the eye away from the small size, awkward proportions or other problems. You might, for instance, create a Mondrian pattern on doors with contrasting colours or set

Left: Surfaces and materials in this kitchen are strictly utilitarian and easy to clean, and the equipment and fittings have been chosen for purely functional reasons, not because they "look right". Yet the bold use of colour and the roller blinds that cover up the big machines cleverly disguise this emphasis on the practical.

The less you see of a colour, the more noticeable it becomes. The combination of natural hardwood and white is now a modern kitchen classic but the addition of black and touches of red adds delightful highlights. Note how the colour of foods and other items soften what might otherwise be a severe room setting.

a panel of tiles behind your hob or cooker containing a large, bold design. You might rack out one wall area, cover it with a collection of utensils, small cookwares, shopping notes, the telephone and shelves containing spice jars, and paint the wall behind the racking in a bold colour which will offset the contents.

You might even consider drawing the eye right out of the kitchen by painting the frame of the main window in a bright colour to highlight the view outside. Or if the view is unattractive but the window is large and centrally placed, why not run open shelves across it and fill them with house plants and cooking herbs? You will still get most of the daylight, diffused through the leaves, and will also have a living feature which is useful, attractive and varies with the seasons.

Another decision to be taken is whether to relate the kitchen in style with adjoining rooms or to make it quite individual. If you want the kitchen to be a restful place, try to link it visually with any spaces with which it is connected, perhaps by shared colour schemes or a floor finish which runs right through. If you wish to achieve a more lively atmosphere, create instead a contrast of colour, texture and mood.

How your kitchen will be lit is very important in two ways. Our perception of space, and especially of how comfortable we feel in it is heavily influenced by how it is lit. A badly-lit room may be full of light surfaces but can still feel dreary to the point of being depressing. Yet you can fill a small room with rich, bold or even vibrant colours and if well-lit, it will be warm, friendly and inviting at all times.

Lighting is something you can really only learn about from experience but the opportunity exists to gain this experience in your own home. Gather together all the movable lights you can find and take them to any room which is already completely decorated and furnished. Wait for a dark evening and then try setting your movable lights in different positions and observe the effects. Point them upwards, downwards and sideways; try them alone and in combinations; see how the atmosphere of the room changes with different settings and note how different light sources make things in the room appear to change colour.

This point about how things change colour when they are lit differently is the second way in which kitchen lighting is important. You may see some furniture in a showroom which looks attractive in a relatively large space and under display lighting. In the quite different setting of a small kitchen, with different light quality and surrounded by different walls and floor surfaces and accessories, the furniture will certainly look quite different as well. It takes long experience to visualize what the change will be, so make sure that you bring together as many of the elements of your proposed design as possible, under the type of lighting you will be using, before ordering any major items.

Lighting in the kitchen can conveniently be thought of as falling into three categories – task, background and occasional. Task lighting is what you need on the worktops and around the sink and hob. The best method to provide this is to fit striplights below cupboards or shelves. Background lighting helps to define the total space but also enables you to see into cupboards. The sources should as far as possible be concealed (see pages 42–43).

Occasional lighting can be used to emphasize particular features in the room at times when you need access but are not actually working there. Even in a very small kitchen it can be used to create an intimate atmosphere for private meals.

Left: One modern technique for differentiating between a kitchen and a living area is to make working surfaces from materials that either are natural or look natural. In this kitchen the break can be made more complete by lowering the Venetian blind to create an intimate dining room. With the blind raised, the whole area becomes a combined family room.

By emphasizing "earth" colours for virtually everything except the fridge, hood, cooker and sink (which is almost hidden anyway, except from the user), this kitchen area has merged into the garden beyond. With modern double glazing this tropical effect could be achieved almost anywhere.

This colour scheme might as easily have been created for a sitting room, bedroom or bathroom. There is no need for the kitchen to appear even remotely utilitarian any longer.

Plants, pine, tiled tops and rough brickwork have become the hallmarks of the "farmhouse revival" style of kitchen. No farmhouse was ever like this, but it is pleasanter to live with than plastic.

Never mind style so long as it works well. There is an increasing rejection of artificially created styles in the kitchen among those who like cooking and don't mind the kitchen looking like a workshop.

Not so much a kitchen, more a way of life. At least it has the advantage that the place will never look untidy, whatever happened there the night before.

When designing interiors you should keep in mind that those who use a room will always add details that become part of the total picture. This is especially true of kitchens. In putting together a complete design scheme you have to accept that you have no control over the style – and the effect – of such things as cornflake packets, cookery books and utensils.

As what matters to most people is the atmosphere of a room when they are actually living and working in it, it is worth planning the design in such a way that the "amiable clutter" which must be part of every kitchen to a greater or lesser extent, is an element in the design.

Much will also depend on whether you wish the furniture to be a strong element in the final design. In real traditional kitchens the furniture was generally austere, functional and almost without decorative features. It was the accessories, utensils and even the food itself which created the "decor" and atmosphere.

For two reasons there is a lot to be said for adopting this approach in today's small kitchens. Firstly, if the furniture itself is not a dominant feature visually the room will in any case appear to be larger. Secondly, if the decor of the room is created with secondary or moveable items, it is easy to change the style to suit new fashions and changes in your own tastes.

Here we consider finishing touches that can be added to a room in which the basic furnishings are simple, functional and low key. The first possibility is to introduce colour, pattern or texture in limited areas with tiling or paintwork. It is worth remembering that, though it is now general practice to tile walls immediately above working areas throughout the kitchen, modern methods of protecting timber and even fabrics mean that you can carry a host of other materials through the room safely and successfully. For instance, if you use wallpaper, paintwork, wood or fabrics on the wall immediately behind a cooking hob, you can easily fix a piece of toughened glass over them to avoid scorching or marking by fat.

The way in which you choose to finish the ceilings and floors will have a quite fundamental effect on the character of the room. We are all conditioned from birth to the "sky father, earth mother" concept and so a room in which the ceiling is light and the floor dark will always feel more comfortable than one in which this scheme of things is reversed.

In any case, it is a mistake to think that making absolutely every part of a small room light will necessarily make it seem larger. So long as there are areas of lightness, especially where you work, the room will feel quite large enough for comfort.

There is an increasing trend towards the use of natural materials such as terracotta tiles, stone and wood for kitchen floors, with throw-down rugs or reed matting added for a touch of softness. Using a natural floor like this in a small kitchen may be all you need to give the design that touch of zest and character.

Alternatively, you can adopt the traditional approach throughout and decorate your kitchen entirely with accessories. There are now many quite delightful ranges of storage jars, pans and utensils which can be used in matching or co-ordinating sets to create particular patterns and focal points in a kitchen layout.

In the early days of fitted kitchens there was a tendency to shut everything away behind doors, mainly as a reaction to the amount of dirt which used to accumulate in kitchens that were not properly ventilated. However, that should no longer be a problem and as items which are in continual use get cleaned anyway, it can be just as practical to store many things in jars and other containers.

On the other hand, there is no reason why a kitchen has to look like a domestic workshop at all. There are examples on these pages that certainly do not. Current fashion colours such as soft pinks, greys, and pretty yellows are used quite as much in kitchen decoration now as they are in any other room in the house.

There is a tendency to use natural materials – wood or stone – for working surfaces and then to choose coloured lacquers or an exotic method of painting for the furniture. Many of the makers of cooking and other equipment, especially AEG-Telefunken, Imperial and Gaggenau, now offer equipment in a wide range of optional colours and styles (or in a style so austere that it fits into almost any setting) so that it is possible to approach the colour planning of the room with little regard to practical constraints.

Two views of "tradition" in the kitchen. (Left) Pine by Smallbone and a terracotta floor by Elon tiles. (Below left) Old Pine by SieMatic teamed with the real thing plus a wood floor and ceiling.

(Above) This kitchen is functionally traditional without attempting to look antique. (Below) Wood and tiles used a different way, with mirrors to create a sense of space where there is none.

FINISHING TOUCHES

There has been a trend over the last twenty years or so for the furniture in a kitchen to be its dominant visual feature but there are now signs of a swing back toward the traditional idea of using carefully chosen accessories or even utensils, equipment and storage jars to create highlights. The fact that small kitchens are quite likely to be combined with other rooms certainly encourages individual ideas about decor in this area.

Special paint finishes, interesting tiling and un-usual materials are just some of these ideas. Another is the use of industrial racking and storage systems, which are not only totally practical in this context but also have a functional beauty of their own to some eyes.

For the future, decor trends will probably split three ways – traditional, exotic and allowing function to dictate form. On this and the opposite page are a selection of kitchens illustrating all these alternatives and in some cases drawing on all three.

If your kitchen has the advantage of an outside light source of a special quality, as in this Californian beach house, the appearance of many of the things it contains will change. For example, even the big commercial gas hob used here ceases to look like the large chunk of metal it would in any other setting.

Above right: Marble and ceramics are again being used in many kitchens. They can appear cold, yet in this informal setting the Spanish plates set off the china sink so that it looks warm and friendly.

In this French kitchen below two ceramic sinks have been set flush into the tiled working surface, each with their own traditionally-styled brass mixer taps. This has created an attractive but ultra-practical area for food preparation and dishwashing.

Here the utensils, chinaware and storage jars give the kitchen a traditional "feel", even though the "look" is entirely modern. This Australian architect-designed kitchen is a good example of the "function dictating form" approach to decor in that

no attempt has been made to disguise the workshop aspect of the room by choosing colourful materials or finishes. Note how the shelf spacings have been carefully adjusted to the size of the contents, so making maximum use of the space available.

This chromed steel display racking makes an excellent dresser-style store for food items and utensils. For novel and inexpensive fittings like this, visit showrooms specializing in shopfitting equipment and materials. Industrial storage suppliers are another possibility.

Below: Hathaway Country Kitchens are among those companies specializing in romantic recreations of traditional kitchen settings. No rural kitchen ever looked quite like this but the effect is certainly pleasing and colourful yet totally practical.

The character of a large urban Victorian building is usually so definite that you may have to go to some lengths to create a visual approach which is powerful enough to match the strength of the kitchen's surroundings. Black Formica worktops and red painted cupboards would probably be too much of a good thing for most people, yet they suit this mansion flat.

Above right: Even the selection of an exotic finish – in this case hand-finished stained birch plywood – has not been allowed to detract from the total practicality of this kitchen, with its maple worktop and wide variety of storage alternatives. The traditional dresser below shows how even some of the oldest ideas still work well in today's kitchens.

SMALL CAN BE BEAUTIFUL

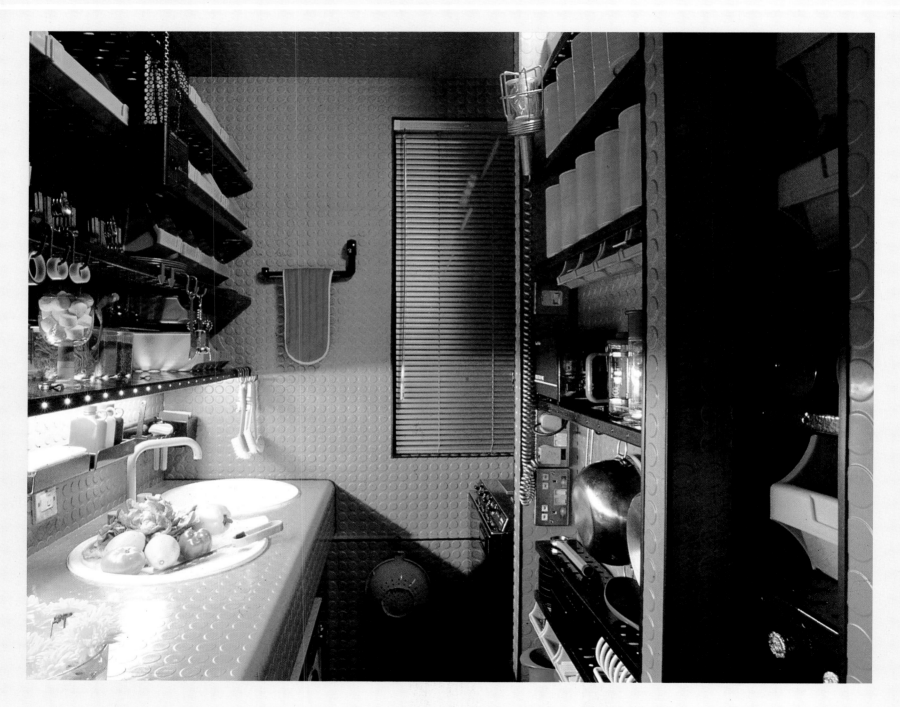

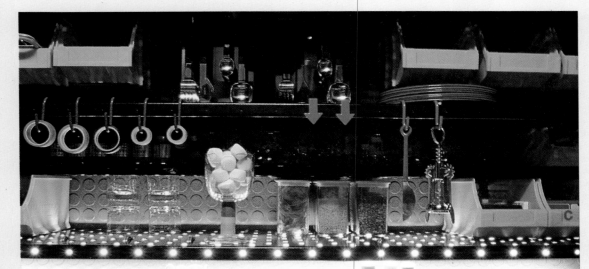

Small kitchens don't have to be dull kitchens. It is often assumed that creating a kitchen in a very small area with little or no natural daylight means that everything has to be as light as possible and that dramatic treatments and bold colours are out of the question.

When she created this kitchen for her own apartment, architect Eva Jiricna broke away from such a conventional approach to produce a startling design which is nonetheless utterly functional. She also showed how contrasting colours can be used as an alternative to pale colours to create a sense of lightness.

The success of the design depends on an unorthodox use of materials and fittings that owes more to workshop design practice than to ideas you would usually expect to see in the home. The green surfaces are dimpled rubber and the shelving system and plastic bins were made with assembly components in mind.

Such a radical visual approach will not appeal to many people, but this design does show how even in a small area there is still room for individuality and flair. And unlike so many visually dramatic kitchens portrayed in glossy magazines, this is an object lesson in functional planning. All the surfaces are easy to clean; everything in regular use comes readily to hand; the wall-strip accessory rack ensures you don't lose small gadgets and the way the over-worktop lighting spills through the bottom shelf to create a visual highlight is little short of brilliant.

Note how the Danish Vola taps, designed by another architect – Arne Jakobson – pick up the colour of the storage bins and how touches of other primary colours introduce visual variety.

Introducing strong colours into a kitchen is always a risk. They may go out of fashion or simply become boring once the novelty has worn off. Here it has been done with such a combination of skill and panache that the design will almost certainly retain its visual freshness indefinitely.

KEEPING IT COOL

A kitchen can look like this only when there is no work going on in it. During meal preparation, these two designs would be as colourfully chaotic as yours or mine, but they do have the advantage that, with the doors closed and the surfaces cleared, everything seems coolly efficient.

In the design on this page there was an awkward shape to overcome – the use of a pale colour means that you are almost unaware of how close the walls are. Access to the fridge and low-level oven calls for agility, but note how practical some of the other details are. The floor, for instance, has its vinyl sheet curved up onto the cupboard plinths to avoid what is usually a bad dirt trap.

Count the number of different tones of white which have been used in the kitchen on page 81. The cabinet handles are a shade different from the doors; the worktops another shade again. The enamel finish of the sink and hob is hard white, as are the taps, but the tiles are cream and the dots give a touch of visual relief that saves the design from becoming too severe.

If you are thinking of designing an "all white" kitchen in this way, you will be tempted to try to match all the materials to one common tone. In practice you will find that lighting variations will defeat you anyway, but these two examples show how well intentional mismatches using compatible shades can work.

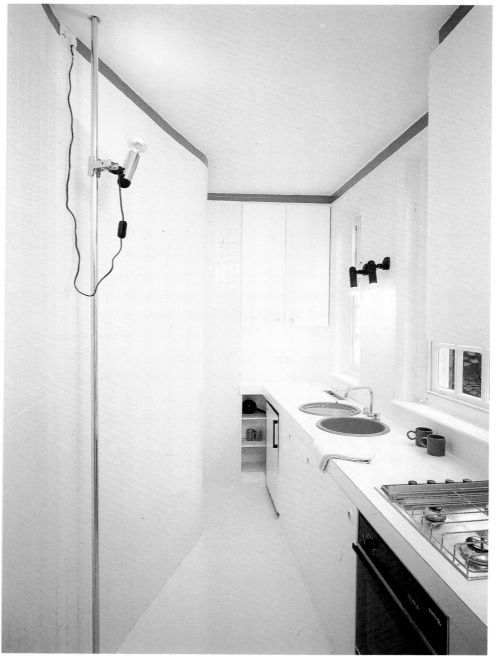

SHAMELESS INDIVIDUALITY

You won't have too much trouble finding anything in any one of these kitchens. All three have been designed first of all as practical working areas with style almost as an afterthought.

Note the subtle differences between the Italian kitchen by Arclinea above and the French design on the right. Both use primary colours to create patterns but the Italian design shows a greater concern with creating different types and sizes of storage for different items.

The interesting thing is that the French kitchen contains more equipment than a first glance reveals. There is not only an oven, gas hob and sink but also a dishwasher under the counter to the left. The oven and fridge in the Italian kitchen are to the left, as the kitchen's eating area, around which it was designed, also doubles as an overspill working surface.

By most people's standards, the kitchen opposite is a potential disaster area, but it is saved from becoming a massive dirt trap by the big central extractor canopy at the top. The layout is in fact entirely practical and very compact. Note that a big sink and a full-size hob have been used and that there is a single oven set in the wall to the left.

RUSTIC CHIC

Here we have another French kitchen but in this case the space was awkward rather than particularly small. Given all this rustic detail some people would have been tempted to recreate a traditional farmhouse setting. Unfortunately the results are so often "over the top".

In this case the design has been tackled with a total lack of self-consciousness and the result is that the kitchen furniture and equipment do not detract visually from the old beams, brickwork and open roofline. The access to

the storage space in the pitch of the roof up a spiral stair is a delightful touch and the use of blue paint, picked up again in chinaware adds a touch of freshness.

The layout of the kitchen itself is absolutely conventional, though the idea of placing the dishwasher and a secondary sink in the centre island is a little unusual. The objective is to enable people to clear the table and dispose of used crockery without getting under the feet of those already in the kitchen working area preparing to serve the next course.

COUNTRY CASUAL

Both these kitchens are in cottages but their designers have approached the objective of creating a relaxed environment for weekend living and holidays in different ways.

Because neither black nor white are colours, they emphasize anything you add to them. The blue floor and accessories and the limestone blocks and pebbles in the kitchen on this page are therefore stronger design elements than they might be otherwise and the whole scheme becomes almost sculptural.

On the far right, worktops of solid maple have been mounted on cupboards made of old pine which recall apothecary's drawers in Victorian dispensaries. You might be tempted to label these to make finding things less of a chore.

The common feature of both designs is the extensive use of white to create a sense of airiness and cleanliness. The painted tongue-and-groove panelling on this page is a practical finish, now used quite often in kitchens for both walls and ceilings as it reflects light well and is easy to keep clean.

In the context of a kitchen, painting rough brickwork leaves the attractive texture and makes the surfaces concerned far easier to maintain. It was for this reason that old kitchens were limewashed; modern resin-based paints are easier to apply and last far longer.

As it happens, steel is enjoying a design revival in Europe now, as the new layout by Bulthaup on this page shows. The chopping block, box drawers and knife rack are of beech, but rails used for towels and hanging pans, the cooker canopy and the utensil rack are all made of steel.

It is also worth noting that this kitchen illustrates the trend away from using plastic laminates for coloured finishes. The anthracite matt lacquer used here is just one of some 50 colour options, ranging from bold primaries to the subtlest pastels, offered by manufacturers.

Black and white emphasize other colours that might appear almost neutral in another setting. Though both these designs are "masculine", the use of wood brings touches of warmth which are repeated in copperware, dried ingredients, terracotta containers and the cork floor opposite.

The kitchen on the left shows how European thinking has influenced the American approach to style. There are strong overtones of both Italian and German style, yet the approach is unmistakably that of the New World. Note the wider worktops in beautifully matured maple and the wide use of stainless steel in high-wear areas.

HI-TECH AND NO NONSENSE

At first glance the kitchen on this page – another design by architect Eva Jiricna – might be confused with a commercial food preparation area, yet once you get away from the "hi-tech" imagery, and the yards of brushed stainless steel, it emerges as a simple and compact domestic design.

Everything is what it appears to be, though you might not realize at first that the working surface is grooved marble with two ceramic cooking rings set in flush to the right. The only point of colour relief is the warm hardwood floor.

On this page, German hi-tech is used in an American setting. The furniture is Zeilodesign Contura by Allmilmö, teamed here with worktops and floor in polished slate. Note the really massive sink of enamelled cast iron – easy to clean and virtually indestructible.

TOUCHES OF COLOUR

There has been no conscious attempt to emphasize design in this kitchen as materials and colours have been chosen mainly for functional reasons, but also simply because the user liked them. The design is austere, but a touch of colour adds essential relief, linking shelf-edges, pans, jars and tea towel.

Unless a colour or a material is very powerful, the more you repeat it in a room, the less you notice it. Here the white and stainless steel disappear and the focus is the touch of red.

Far right, this page: A strong pattern created by emphasizing tile joints dominates the white furniture and stainless steel equipment in this kitchen. The emphasis is achieved by grouting plain tiles in a contrasting colour, such as red or black. The effect is to relieve an otherwise bland design. Such small touches of colour as the split reed blind, the cane basket and the fruit and vegetables appear as strong design elements, whereas in most kitchens you would probably not notice them.

Rustic simplicity is the keynote of this tiny cooking area. Because it is in a weekend cottage, there is no need for a complete kitchen: this area is as practical as possible within such a limited space. Most important of all, it does not detract from the character of the surrounding building. Any attempt to pretty it up with more elaborate furniture, or stronger colours for the sink and other fittings, would have ruined the delicate balance which has been achieved in blending the area in with the surrounding rough stonework.

STAINLESS STEEL STYLE

Colour has been eliminated as far as possible from this tiny kitchen and yet plays an essential role in a layout that is full of carefully-thought out details. The use of the deep blue tiles to define the cooking area cleverly draws the eye away from the light pelmet above and relieves an otherwise oppressive wall. The repetition of brushed steel and aluminium gives these materials the characteristics of a colour. Note the use-ful pull-out surface below the fridge and oven which solves the problem of where to serve up a meal and provides a use-ful secondary mixing and food preparation area that slides out of the way during laundering. The kettle is kept permanently on the ceramic hob. One advantage of a ceramic hob is that the surface can be used for other purposes when all or part of it is not being used for cooking.

At first sight these three kitchens appear completely unplanned visually, yet in fact great care has gone into select- *ing colours, materials and textures that create specific atmospheres. A key factor in this is deciding what to omit.*

In the kitchen on the left there is so little colour to detract from the maple surfaces and wood strip walls that, despite the wide use of metals in equipment, utensils and fittings, they become the dominant features.

The designer of the kitchen below did not have the advantage of a large space to work in so, though similar thoughts on colour were followed, detail and pattern had to be added. The slatted shelves and the exotic woods used for the end surface and flank wall provide just the visual relief required.

Because blue crops up so often in traditional china-ware it has become a classic colour in kitchens. However, the kitchen above is also traditional in the way in which it is the contents – the utensils, storage jars, china, pans and ingredients – that form the decor, not the furniture or the wall finishes.

WHITE FOR DISCRETION

Intrusive pipework is a problem in many kitchens but few of us have to cope with anything quite as bad as this! Yet the use of white paint throughout has neutralized the obtrusiveness of the pipes, and the arrangement of working areas and storage means that the big vertical duct appears to fall at a relatively convenient point in the room. In practice however it must have taken careful planning to achieve this effect.

This arrangement uses much the same colour elements as the kitchen opposite yet, despite the white floor, it appears warmer because several of the contents, such as the espresso machine and the books, have been allowed to become colour elements in the design. In an austere setting like this, colour has to be used with great discretion. Imagine, for instance, how out of place a set of patterned enamel saucepans would look on the vertical chromed steel hanging rack.

UNORTHODOX STYLE

Not one item of orthodox kitchen furniture has been used in this room, yet a strong sense of style has been created by adopting an industrial perforated metal drawer system for much of the storage. Both the layout and the patterns created by the fittings and their contents have been planned down to the smallest detail.

The most straightforward free-standing equipment and fittings have been used in this kitchen, even down to a swing-lid waste bin (though note the chains used to deter flies). Great care has been taken with the over-all colour scheme, and the use of matt black for cupboard doors and iron grey for the worktop means that the cookery books, fruit and flowers create a decor which changes with the seasons.

VIVE LA DIFFERENCE

When you consider that all kitchens are used for more or less the same purposes and, give or take a few items, have to contain much the same pieces of equipment, it really is remarkable how people manage to stamp their own identities upon them. The French design on this page relegates the kitchen to little more than a sideboard with a sink and hobs set in it whereas the American design opposite is an exuberant celebration of the delights of cooking for pleasure. The link between these two designs is that a large cupboard is used in both to solve the main storage problem. The French kitchen area becomes "invisible" when not in use because one material has been used overall.

The big fridge-freezer and foodstore which make up the remainder of this American kitchen are out of shot, but just about everything else can be seen. The space occupied by the kitchen is quite small – it appears larger because of the distortion inevitable in a picture taken with a wide-angle lens – but it contains full-size commercial cooking equipment.

The principle behind the planning of this kitchen is that just about everything, apart from food items and large pans, which are in the cupboards below the working surface, is kept in the central store. When food is being prepared you bring what equipment you need to the surface where you are working, use it, and move on to the next stage. The same principle is used in planning commercial kitchens.

If you have to create a kitchen area at one end of a fairly tall room in a period house, this is certainly one way to do it successfully. Materials and colours which would not have been associated with the kitchen a few years ago have here been used in a kitchen that is thoroughly practical without being in the least utilitarian.

The wood used is clear Douglas Fir, which is much more satisfactory than the knotty pine which is a more common choice. Douglas Fir is somewhat harder and much less prone to twisting and cracking. However, all softwoods will shrink, sometimes quite dramatically, when subjected to central heating and most will darken considerably with time.

The choice of fir for the main worktop is one which the owner may regret in time. The wood has been varnished, but this will not protect it for long from cutting damage or heat marks.

Oddly enough, using a woven carpet is quite practical and a good way of overcoming the problems that might arise if anything were spilt on bare boards. There are now a number of proprietary materials available to protect carpets, curtain fabrics and blinds from practically any form of spillage or spattering in the kitchen.

The layout has been cleverly planned so that the big fridge-freezer and the nearby shelving cannot be seen from the eating area. Note that the extractor canopy runs straight up to the ceiling. In older buildings like this there is often enough space in the void between the ceiling and the floor above to run a duct from such an extractor out between the joists.

This room follows the traditional approach to decor – apart from the richness of the natural wood, all the colour is in added detail and the foods and utensils in the working area.

VISUAL IMPACT

In these kitchens the marriage between the practical and the visual is highly individual and yet successful, though in quite different ways. The yellow and grey colour scheme on this page has been carried through from the sitting area very simply. If orthodox cupboards had been used for the main storage instead of open industrial racking, the visual impression would have been too bland. As it is, the kitchen area has been created with a minimum of expense and much of the furniture can easily be moved on to the next apartment.

Arrangements like this are ideal for bachelors and couples. Note how a multi-purpose surface has been cleverly created to the right of the sink. It can be used as an extension of the food preparation area, for serving up meals which may also be eaten there or taken over to the sitting area, or for stacking crockery before washing.

A small peninsula like this also makes a practical division between the working and living areas in a house or apartment where parties or gatherings of friends are likely to be commonplace.

The French kitchen above was designed with permanent residence in mind and follows a trend that is becoming stronger all the time. Strictly functional materials and finishes, such as the stainless steel used in this kitchen, are chosen for working surfaces and equipment, yet it is the colours selected for the cabinets and room door which dominate.

The link between these two kitchens is that they obey the rule that is central to so much good modern interior design. The impact is achieved by eliminating all but two or three colour tones; white, black and polished metal then effectively become neutrals.

The kitchen offers an interesting alternative to open shelves or closed cupboards. The wide use of obscured glass means that even a stranger to the room would have little difficulty finding anything, yet the contents do not detract from the crispness of the design as they would have if open shelves had been used.

CASE HISTORY 1

INTRODUCTION

The designs shown in this section were created to meet quite specific personal requirements. Though the kitchens are small in relation to the work done in them, or the number of people who use them, their owners are delighted with the results both in practical and visual terms. In several of the kitchens a compact design was deliberately chosen even though more space could easily have been made available.

Some of the kitchens are owned by designers or people who write about cookery or kitchen design. Interestingly, the designs are neither extreme nor do they incorporate unusual equipment or materials. The ways in which everyday requirements are met would work equally well in any other kitchen planned to meet similar needs.

The common factor that links these designs, apart from compact layout, is the care that has been taken in the choice of equipment and working surfaces and in the design of storage facilities. The evident concern for style or atmosphere has not been allowed to take precedence over the need to create a room that works efficiently and harmoniously in a limited space.

Perhaps the most challenging part of kitchen design is achieving a successful balance between the practical and visual aspects of the job. It should not be a question of compromise. In the best designs, each of these aspects actually contributes to the success of the other, though where the emphasis should lie will be a matter of individual choice.

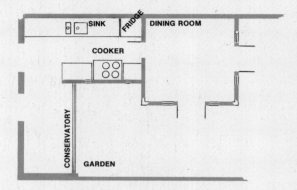

Technical information

Designers Conklin Rossant Partnership
20 Park Avenue South, New York 10003.
Floors and worktops Of pink and cream marble throughout.
Cooking equipment Commercial gas range and "salamander" grill.
Refrigeration Traulsen domestic model. In the main Traulsen make commercial refrigeration equipment.
Dishwasher Thermador all-stainless steel semi-commercial model.
Food processing Built-in Nutone Food Center.
Lighting The scheme can be varied.
Main lighting is by angled downlighters, but special striplights are concealed in the pyramid-shaped ceilings to provide background illumination in the kitchen area when the dining room is being used.

A cookery writer's kitchen in New York

Jim Rossant is an architect who enjoys designing interiors and especially kitchens. His wife Colette is a writer on cookery. So when they decided radically to alter the kitchen and dining area at the rear of their brick-built Federal-style town house in SoHo, Lower Manhattan, the stage was set for an interesting interplay of ideas.

The kitchen was to be used as much for working – the creation and testing of dishes, such as those in Mrs Rossant's book *Colette's Japanese Cuisine* – as for preparing family meals. However, the Rossants have four grown-up children and three of these frequently get involved in cooking in the kitchen as well.

The design had to meet all these practical requirements as well as to satisfy Jim Rossant's strong sense of style. The interesting thing is that, though there was ample space to create a much larger kitchen, it was deliberately decided to make the actual working area compact, using further space in the adjoining hall to store items which are relatively rarely used and so need not be immediately to hand in the kitchen.

The house was extended at the rear toward the garden to create a new area for the kitchen itself and also to add a square dining room, which is approached through the kitchen. In the picture to the right, the curved conservatory roof covers a balcony which as well as being the approach to the garden also stores part of Colette Rossant's collection of classic cooking pans. The main kitchen working area is in the small square in the centre and the dining room is below the copper dome to the right.

The unusual pattern on the exterior of the kitchen wall is seated by two small windows set either side of the cooking range and giving views out to the gardens, and by a round outlet between them for the fumes and smoke from a commercial "salamander" (a giant gas grill) which is set above the main cooker.

The kitchen is intentionally integrated closely into the house as a whole and the decision to approach the dining room through the kitchen was deliberate. The Rossants entertain a good deal and like to involve their guests to some extent in their own enthusiasm for cookery. However, the dining room has its own quite distinct character as it has windows on all four sides, which gives the pleasing impression of eating in the garden, especially attractive on a mild summer's evening.

In such a compact arrangement colours and textures have to be used with great restraint. Marble and stainless steel are used for most surfaces and for the finishes on the equipment, with the decor created by the geometry of the spaces and furniture and by the colours, shapes and textures of the racks of utensils.

This brick-built Federal-style house in an area of Lower Manhattan near Greenwich Village known as SoHo dates from approximately 1832. This part of New York is largely occupied by artists, writers and other creative people and its character was reflected in the stylish design of the additions that now house the new kitchen and dining areas. The outlook is toward a narrow but quite long garden and a feature of the design is that, by fitting windows all round, the dining room appears to be part of this garden area. The domed roof of the dining room is of copper and additional light is admitted through glass bricks set into the upper corners.

A view through the main working area towards the dining room. To the left a large but conventional double sink is flanked by the all-stainless steel Thermador dishwasher on one side and a built-under freezer on the other. At the end is the large commercial-style multi-zone refrigerator. To the right a large marble pastry-making area has the motor of the Nutone Food Center set flush into it near the cooker. This in turn is a commercial gas range with a big "salamander" grill set above. You can just see one of the two small windows which give the cook a view out to the garden beyond.

All the cabinets in this kitchen were individually made of stainless steel and lined with rubber sheeting for quietness. Most utensils are kept out on racks for immediate access and Colette Rossant's big set of traditional tin-lined copper saucepans creates visual echoes that go back to a century or more before Mrs. Beaton.

CASE HISTORY 1

Many keen cooks now use commercial cooking equipment rather than domestic built-in ovens and hobs, but such appliances do create special problems when planning ventilation. In this kitchen the outlet from the big canopy above the cooking range was made into a feature on the exterior of the kitchen by forming it in brick between the two small windows.

Perhaps the most spectacular feature of the building extension is this balcony which leads to the garden with its conservatory-style curved roof. The pan racking spills over into this area from the kitchen itself, but is still easily accessible, and the copper of the pans themselves becomes a strong element in the design. You can guess that in time this area will provide a winter haven for house plants and possibly for hanging baskets of herbs.

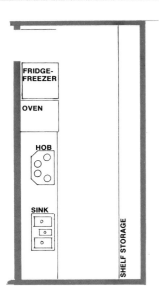

Technical information

Designers Woodstock Butcherblock Furniture Ltd, Packenham Street, Mount Pleasant, London WC1X 0LB.
Floor and wall tiles Mexican terracotta tiles imported by Woodstock
Furniture and worktops Individually designed and made in solid maple by Woodstock
Sink Franke Compact stainless steel three-bowl, with fitted chopping block and draining basket (not shown)
Hob Scholtes gas
Oven AEG-Telefunken UK Ltd, double electric oven

Doing the impossible with real style.

One interesting feature of the British kitchens' market at present is the increasing number of specialized designer/makers who have become established in recent years. Among the leaders in this movement are Woodstock in Mount Pleasant, London, run by the husband and wife team of Wendy and Alf Martensson.

They have created kitchens that are very much in the traditional idiom without making any attempt to ape particular period styles. Each of their designs reflects a combination of Wendy Martensson's background in North America and Alf Martensson's in Norway, creating a particular mix of elegance and craftsmanship which is both unique and timeless.

All Woodstock designs use wood, and particularly solid maple, with style and panache and the illustrations show how this can be achieved in even the most unlikely situations. This design also encapsulates just about everything which is best about the latest thinking on the planning and equipping of small kitchens.

It was made for a journalist and his family in an extension to the existing house, as the old kitchen area, even smaller, was considered totally inadequate. The old way to tackle a space like this would have been to set a narrow worktop down both sides, which would have meant continual twisting and turning from one side to the other plus ducking and reaching for food items and utensils. Instead, Woodstock concentrated most storage on open shelves on one side and then created an uncluttered working area on the other, with those pans and kitchenwares in constant use hung on wall racking above for instant and easy accessibility.

The temptation to add wall cupboards was avoided because they would have accentuated the narrowness of the space. Instead, concealed lighting has been set below a high-level shelf to ensure that there is good working light at all times, always from the same direction whether there is daylight from the glazed roof or not. Incidentally, Woodstock designed the attractive extension as well as the kitchen within it.

The richness of both the wall and floor tiles complements the natural tones of the maple cupboards, worktop, wall racking and open shelves and keeping the colours of the fittings and equipment simple (stainless steel or white) prevented the overall effect becoming fussy.

The main equipment items chosen are also classics of their type. The sink is the stainless steel Franke Compact in its three-bowl guise: the original version, introduced some years ago, has been much copied but is still the best design of its type. The sickle-shaped Scholtes four-ring gas hob has been on the market for more than a decade, but still offers a unique layout which has proved popular with keen cooks in both Europe and North America.

The double oven is by AEG-Telefunken, with cooking by hot air in the main oven and by radiant grill in the secondary oven above. The combined fridge-freezer is from the same company. Again, the choices have fallen on robust, proven designs which have a good track record for performance and reliability.

This could so easily have been a very unpleasant space to work in but designer/makers Woodstock have brought their special touch to the lay-out and colour scheme. As a result it is an excellent example of how sound solutions to functional problems can be achieved while also creating a friendly and elegant working environment. In particular, this kitchen also exemplifies how planning a small kitchen vertically works far better than the old "working triangle" approach. It ensures that, wherever you are working, everything you need is readily to hand without any bending, stretching or ducking round doors.

The temptation to tile the wall in white or a neutral shade was resisted and the alternative chosen has many of the visual advantages of a mirror, in that when working in this area you are hardly aware of how close the wall really is. Ventilation is achieved through a high-level extractor which ensures that the whole area is kept reasonably clean at all times. Without that and with a large gas hob, the choice of so much open shelf storage would have been ill-advised.

The spacing of many of the wall shelves can be varied so that over the years, as needs and contents change, the owners can still make every inch count. The use of oiled maple throughout means that every surface is washable. In practice this material is as easy to look after as plastic, but it ages far more gracefully.

CASE HISTORY 3

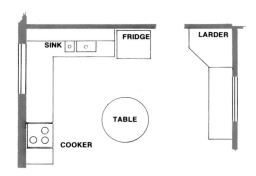

Technical information

Designers The owners
Floor Random limestone slabs
Working surfaces Partly white plastic laminates but also stainless steel with moulded-in sink. Available in UK through Dahl-Scandia
Cooker Husqvarna
Cooker Hood Futura (Exactum in UK)

A casual lesson in good design

At first sight this kitchen, which is in a Swedish holiday home, looks as if it was allowed to evolve quite casually without too much thought being given to the practical details. Yet when you look more closely it is an object lesson in good design and, with a few minor changes, would be quite suitable for fulltime family use.

There are two ways to look at this layout. It contains all the elements of a truly traditional kitchen, apart from a big central working table and that could easily be added. There is a large sink, a big food storage cupboard and open shelf storage for those items most often used.

Yet if you look at the details, the design also matches the thesis that for maximum efficiency storage should be concentrated between hip and shoulder height, with emphasis on a big fridge and a big foodstore to concentrate lots of capacity in a small floor area.

Starting at the cooking end of the kitchen, there is a heatproof top of stone to the left of the cooker, essential if you are using a solid-plate cooking hob because if something is about to boil over the only way to stop it is to take the pan off the hotplate till it has cooled down a little. The resting position on the hob is logically used, as shown here, as a home for the kettle. Three hotplates might not be adequate for a large family, but a microwave oven could easily be added at a later date.

Most utensils are stored in the run of drawers below the worktops around the cooker and sink and the deep windowsill is used as an overspill storage area. The sink itself is moulded into a continuous stainless steel working surface which doubles as a draining board. The actual draining rack above folds up when not in use so that the worktop below is then completely clear for use as a food preparation area, with the fridge and freezer set conveniently just to the right.

The open shelving above has been carefully planned so that the shelves are no deeper than their contents nor spaced further apart than strictly necessary. The wood strip immediately below them was fitted there so that hooks could be screwed in for hanging utensils and gadgets, such as the draining rack which is already there. The secret to spacing shelves like this is to set the bottom shelf as low as practical and then put the next two or three shelves as close as possible, concentrating on

storing small items on them. Larger items can then be stored at the higher levels where they will still be quite accessible.

The second worktop area, next to the big store cupboard (which the owners say was designed to be mouseproof when the house is unoccupied), is mainly used for assembling snack meals. Table cutlery is stored in the drawers; the napkins are ready to hand and there is even a space for the trolley, which can be brought into use to take serving dishes to the dining area during major meals. The centre table and seats are used for snacks and also as a point to which dirty dishes can be brought without cluttering the sink area.

The materials used in the kitchen blend into the original room setting as they repeat colours and textures which were already there – limestone flags, brick, white plaster and pine. In this context stainless steel, used in the sink area and for the ventilation duct above, becomes a neutral.

Simple but carefully thought out, the top next to the cooker is a spare piece of limestone flooring and therefore heatproof. The wire shelf racks can be taken to the sink for washing. There is a resting place for the kettle, when not in use, on this three-ring hob.

This casual kitchen layout is deceptive in the sense that it merges well into the character of the old building it occupies yet has been planned with great care to be efficient in use. Because this is a holiday home, a recirculating cooker hood is adequate. The type shown here is by Swedish makers Futura and contains a simple plastic matrix filter which lasts for the life of the machine and can be rinsed out at the sink. If this were a family house a proper extractor would be essential to prevent dirt staining the bare boards and beams above.

CASE HISTORY 3

Careful planning of the shelf depths and spacings means that every inch is used to maximum effect and every item has its proper place. The draining rack folds up to leave the worktop below clear for food preparation.

This secondary area is useful for preparing breakfasts and snacks. Table cutlery is stored in the drawers below the worktop and the trolley below is used to carry serving dishes to the dining table. All long-term storage is concentrated in the big corner cupboard, apart from chinaware and the food in the fridge-freezer.

CASE HISTORY 4

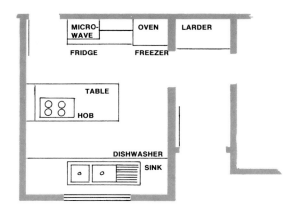

Technical information

Designer R.M. Murrell

Furniture and worktops Furniture individually made of Douglas fir, finished with liquid wax. Worktops of oiled solid maple.

Sink The Pallas model by Villeroy and Boch, made of Asterite in pearl grey. Accessories include a draining rack and chopping block

Taps Czech & Speake 1910

Waste disposer ISE 77

Dishwasher Fully-integrated AEG-Telefunken Favorit 525i

Hob AEG-Telefunken B60L Quattro multifunction oven and grill

Secondary oven Brother combined microwave/hot air cooker

Fridge & Freezer Philips

Cottage kitchen for a growing family

Bran End is a small cottage in an English village near the Hertfordshire/Essex border 35 miles north of London. The owners have two children who will shortly be in their teens and therefore likely to spend an increasing amount of time in the kitchen. With cooking quite often a shared activity, it was clear that the kitchen would have to be re-modelled to meet these new requirements.

The original plan was to create an extension at the back of the existing building and move the kitchen out into it. However, after much discussion, it was decided that if a satisfactory new kitchen lay-out could be achieved in the existing space, the extension would be used as a dining and garden room instead. The advantage would be that the kitchen would then remain in the heart of the house, which was more appropriate to the way it was used. The snag was that it would often have to contain four people, each of whom might be "doing their own thing".

Having taken the decision not to move the kitchen, the main problems were to fit a full range of equipment in the room and to isolate the main working area from "traffic" passing through from the front of the house to the dining room or out into the garden.

The solution was to create a central working/eating/serving area dividing the room into a primary work zone – containing the sink, dishwasher and hob – and a secondary zone containing the oven, microwave, fridge and freezer.

The small working/serving area is shared between the surrounding items of equipment and the design is successful because it will be rare for people to be actively working at both ovens and the fridge and freezer simultaneously. In any case, it is only half a step from either oven to the central table area if more space is needed. In practice the table is mostly used to assemble and serve meals which are to be taken to the adjoining dining room.

In the limited space available, the sizes of working areas and of the centre table in particular had to be calculated carefully. Several surfaces are dual purpose and the hob chosen was a special model which is set completely flush in the table top, so that it can be covered by a cloth at mealtimes or when required for some purpose other than cooking.

The furniture was individually made in Douglas fir in a traditional style to suit the age and character of the cottage, and all the working surfaces are of solid maple with a simple oiled finish. A classic blue and white colour scheme was chosen for the decor and, because the kitchen is also used by pets, the floor was tiled in a neutral shade chosen for easy maintenance.

A considerable amount of storage space was gained by creating a large ventilated larder in the lobby immediately outside the kitchen where it is readily accessible from either of the working areas. The result is that it is quite practical for snacks and breakfast to be prepared on the farther side of the kitchen while a major meal is being completed in the main area.

This view across the main working area and centre working/eating table towards the oven and microwave and their shared worktop makes the kitchen appear larger than it actually is. However, by careful calcula- tion of the spacings and surface sizes it was pos- sible to fit four people and a good deal of equip- ment into a smaller area than appeared practical at first. The controls for the hob are set in the hanging rack above.

As is so often the case with small kitchens, the key to the layout was concentrating a great deal of the storage re- quired into one compact cupboard. The ventilated larder was sited in a lobby just outside the main kitchen area but easily accessible to any- one preparing meals or snacks.

CASE HISTORY 5

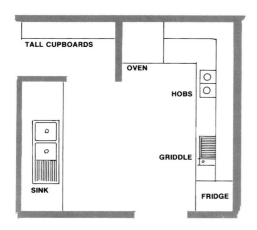

TALL CUPBOARDS
OVEN
HOBS
GRIDDLE
SINK
FRIDGE

Technical information

Designers Robin Guild Associates, 107a Pimlico Road, London SW1
Kitchen furniture By Boffi in bleached ash veneer.
Worktops Also by Boffi in Rosa Dante granite.
Sink Pland stainless steel
Hobs Jenn-Air electric griddle and downdraught extractor; White-Westinghouse twin gas hobs.
Oven American Westinghouse double oven.
Floor Wicanders Cork-o-Plast tiling.

Simply international

Compared with a decade or so ago, even the most straightforward kitchen designs are now likely to be international in the sense that furniture, equipment and decor items may come from a number of different countries. Certainly in the western world we now take it for granted that we can choose the best which is available from more or less anywhere in the world to create a kitchen setting. Consequently when an internationally famous designer sets about renovating a kitchen for his own use it is hardly surprising that the sources of supply for both materials and equipment are so diverse.

The kitchen illustrated here was created by Robin Guild's own design company for his Kensington, London, Georgian mews house and its visual austerity probably owes as much to his views on in-

terior design as it does to batchelor usage. The layout was largely dictated by the limitations of the building, yet it was still possible to establish a feeling of relaxed stylishness without cutting any corners in the selection of some very capable cooking equipment drawn from both Europe and North America.

The furniture is by Italian trend-setters Boffi, finished in bleached ash, and the Rosa Dante granite worktops come from the same country. So does the combined refrigerator and freezer. However, the Jenn-Air electric griddle (fitted with its own integral smoke extractor) and the Westinghouse rings and double oven are all American made.

The double stainless steel sink on the opposite side of the room is British, as are the straighforward chromed mixer taps. No doubt the cork for the floor originally came from Spain but the tile system is an exceedingly practical combination of cork and vinyl made by the British company Wicanders and called Cork-o-Plast.

Designs like this are deceptive in their simplicity. Consider, for instance, how the appearance of this room would have been changed if the walls around the working areas had been tiled in the conventional way. Instead Robin Guild opted to use Red Cedar panelling (from Canada), proofed with a clear emulsion finish. The effect is both striking and unusual.

In fact this wall finish had been used extensively elsewhere in the house and so forms a visual link between adjoining areas. Yet the vertical character which it gives to the kitchen area specifically creates a sense of height in a small space and the fact that the colour of this wood is stronger than that in the doors draws the eyes to the limits of the room rather than towards the furniture, again giving a sense of greater space. The overall effect is of style combined with practicality.

A pull-out table surface creates an additional area for assembling meals but is more often used for quick snacks. The wood panelling has been proofed to protect it from water splashing up from the sink.

A secondary area of dry goods storage has been created in tall shallow cupboards to the left in a lobby. The projecting wall to the left of the oven ensures that anyone entering the room will not clash with a hot door.

CASE HISTORY 6

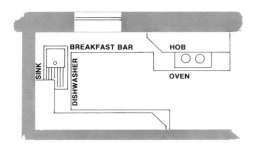

Technical details

Designers Woodgoods, High Street, Odiham, Hants RG25 1LN
Furniture Individually made in recycled pine by Woodgoods
Working surfaces and wall tiling Glazed terracotta tiles by Woodgoods, with old pine worktop edging
Oven, hob, washer and canopy extractor Philips
Sink Ceramic sink by Villeroy & Boch
Floor Vinyl sheet flooring in tile effect

A cottage kitchen for two

The ways in which we use our kitchens are continually changing. The most recent changes are that we now expect to get a great deal more equipment into them than ever before and the range of foods stored in most kitchens is also now considerable. The result is, particularly in older houses, that spaces that might once have been adequate are now inadequate.

The solution often chosen is to extend the building and sometimes, especially where cooking for a growing family is involved, that solution may be the only satisfactory one. However, if the house is a small cottage there is a real danger of spoiling its proportions and layout. Only two people occupy this cottage so it was possible to use ingenious design to fit what they needed into the existing space.

The cottage is in Hampshire, to the south-west of London, and local designer/makers Woodgoods created the furniture and fittings. They specialize in designing kitchens in old pine for the owners of hundreds of period houses in that part of England and for those with modern properties who are trying to recapture the traditional atmosphere.

In fact, this type of kitchen is completely modern in the way in which it works and though traditional materials are used wherever possible, their application is modern as well. For instance, the sink is ceramic, but a modern one made by Villeroy & Boch. Old-style glazed terracotta tiles from France and Mexico are used for the working surfaces and walls, even though tiles like this would never have been used in this way in any kitchen a century or more ago.

If you are going to include an oven, hob and a washing machine in limited space some care has to be taken to ensure that there are adequate working surfaces but still enough room to move around safely. The solution is to vary the depths of the worktops, leaving enough to work on yet keeping the spacing between them satisfactory.

The central floor area is just about the smallest space in which a person could work and swing round comfortably and safely, bearing in mind that you have to bend down to deal with the washing machine to the left. To the right, the choice of a built-under oven means that for safe access there has to be a larger area of clear floor in front of it than would be the case with a waist-level oven. The built-under option was chosen to avoid making the kitchen area appear even smaller.

The furniture is in the "stripped pine" style in which just about every aspect of the decor uses neutrals and earth colours. It makes only passing references to real period originals but its immense popularity shows just how strongly the current preoccupation with a search for our cultural roots has influenced thinking about design in kitchens.

Roll-out storage for pans ensures there is access to these everyday items without bending in a narrow space.

The breakfast area below the window doubles as a food preparation area at other times. There is just space for two to work comfortably here.

The decision to fit the kitchen into the available space meant that compromises over worktop depths were essential if sufficient room was to be left for safe movement. Note how the lefthand side of the kitchen is devoted almost entirely to storage. The true working areas have been concentrated at the end around the sink and to the right where the cooker is sited. As the kitchen is used by only two people, the same working area can be utilized for different purposes at different times, with the central space below the window alternating between food preparation, serving, and breakfasting.

CASE HISTORY 7

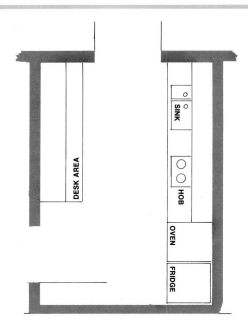

Technical details

Designer Roma Jay Interiors
Furniture Ariston in white laminate finish throughout but with racks, handles and midway shelf in green, mainly of plastic-coated metal
Worktops and sink Of solid Corian with the double sink moulded into the continuous surface
Hob Four-ring electric by Gaggenau
Oven Double oven by Ariston
Fridge-freezer Colston-Ariston
Flooring Cork-o-Plast tiling by Wicanders

By one writer for another

Italian designers and manufacturers have been influential during the past two decades in practically every aspect of design. As far as kitchens are concerned, their influence has been seen mostly in details and ideas on colour rather than in entire settings of furniture and equipment.

Ariston is a company which has had more success than most in selling Italian design. When Roma Jay, who is both a practising designer and writer on the subject, was asked to create a kitchen for a friend who is a cookery writer and broadcaster, they chose the full Ariston treatment to produce the effect illustrated here.

The highlight of this particular kitchen is the limited use of one strong colour against a white background. This idea spawned a whole series of copies at the time when Ariston introduced it, including the red-plus-white designs which subsequently came out of German and British factories in such profusion. Yet none of these had the delicacy of treatment of the original, where the feature colour was confined to plastic-coated metalwork used for the door handles, the midway baskets and the narrow midway shelf.

The house is typically Victorian. In restoring the outside of the building great care was taken to ensure authenticity, but inside the rooms all reflect the best in contemporary design. Ariston was chosen for the kitchen because at the time it was one of the few makers offering a complete package of equipment and furniture which was completely integrated visually. This particular design is no longer available, but it is generally recognized as a classic of its type.

The first stage in the design was to move the kitchen from the basement of the house into what had been a sitting room. This brought it more into the heart of the house and fitted in better with its use as an area for recipe-testing and photography as well as family cooking. The touches of green and the brightness of the total setting also form an excellent link with the small and attractive garden beyond.

Apart from the Gaggenau four-position electric hob, all of the equipment in the kitchen is by Ariston. The worktops are of solid Corian throughout, with double sinks moulded into the continuous surface. A visual link is formed with the adjoining areas in the use of Wicanders Cork-o-Plast for the floor. This unusual tiling, made by sandwiching cork between layers of vinyl, is increasingly popular for kitchen use because it is easy to maintain and keep clean.

At first glance this is a galley kitchen in the old style, but note that the sink, hob and oven have all been placed on one side, so that there is never a danger of bumping into anyone while carrying a hot pan across the room. This side is used for serving, getting breakfast or snacks or for writing at the desk overhang.

This particular furniture design by Ariston of Italy was the forerunner of current thinking on making fuller use of the midway space between worktops and wall cupboards. It used coloured racks to improve access to small items and utensils. The cleaner look created was particularly appropriate in this kitchen because the room was also designed to be used for professional cookery photography.

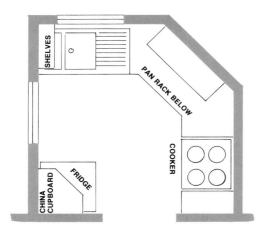

Technical details

Designer The owner
Furniture Individually made of solid American ash with an oiled finish
Worktops White laminate with solid ash edgings
Floor Sealed cork tiles
Cooker and Grill Cannon gas
Refrigeration Gas-fuelled fridge
Sink Double stainless steel

Individualizing an awkward corner

If you are creating an extension to house a kitchen the ideal approach is to plan the kitchen first and then design the extension to fit around it. However, this ideal is rarely possible and quite often a whole series of compromises have to be examined and then resolved.

This kitchen is in an apartment in a Georgian building. The apartment occupies the first and second floors in the house. The old kitchen had to be moved out of the second floor to make room for a second bedroom and space had to be created on the first floor for a new kitchen.

Not only did the new kitchen extension have to fit in with the plans of the occupant of the ground floor apartment, it was discovered that the ideal shape would deprive the neighbouring house of daylight. To avoid that a wall had to be built at an angle across one corner.

The apartment's owner does a good deal of entertaining so, despite the physical constraints, the kitchen had to be thoroughly practical. At the same time the informal and relaxed character of the apartment and the owner's love of antiques and traditional materials needed to be reflected in the overall design.

The owner had such strong personal feelings about how the job should be done that she decided to supervise both the design and installation herself. Coincidentally, her grandmother had been an innovative kitchen designer in the 1930's, interested in the applications of new materials such as stainless steel and a pioneer of kitchens with working surfaces at one level.

Though the kitchen appears to be orthodox at first sight, there are personal touches responsible for its particular character. The most noticeable of these is the pan trolley, which was specially made up from stainless steel shopfitting components by Slingsby of Bradford. The racks can be adjusted, should this ever be necessary, and the trolley is fitted with special castors for ease of movement in the limited space.

The main furniture was made by local craftsmen of specially selected American ash, and oiled rather than waxed to simplify cleaning and to reduce the risk of staining. The wood, the style and the finish were chosen to be in sympathy with a number of antique pine items arranged elsewhere in the room.

The double stainless steel sink and drainer were salvaged from the previous kitchen. The cooker is an old Cannon gas appliance with foldaway high-level grill and plate-warming rack. To ensure silent running, the fridge is also gas-fuelled. The old wooden plate rack next to the cooker is used to store special items, including part of a collection of antique china.

The specially made movable pan trolley was created to the owner's design out of stainless steel shopfitting components. Even pans kept at the back are easy to reach.

The combination of cupboards and open shelves ensures that everything is close at hand wherever you are in this compact kitchen. The shape actually improves accessibility.

The high level gas grill on this old Cannon cooker is still available as a separate item to run on either mains or bottled gas. The old wood rack is for antique plates.

COOKING AND EATING COMBINED

The idea of siting a fully operational kitchen in one part of a room in which you also dine, relax, watch television and perhaps even sleep is becoming commonplace, even in family houses, and also practical.

The most important practical problem to be overcome is ventilation. Simply using a powerful extractor is not the answer. There must be some allowance for an intake of fresh air as well, otherwise you will be saddled with a noisy fan and the loss of a great deal of expensively-heated air from the living area. Next you must ensure that any equipment which is to be installed will operate silently or at noise levels which will not disturb other occupants of the room. You should also attempt to design the kitchen area in such a way that the equipment – the sink, taps, hob and oven – are either unobtrusive or disappear when not in use.

The big step forward has been in furniture design and the total integration of much equipment into the furniture styling, either by colour co-ordination or using furniture panels to conceal the equipment. Many manufacturers of kitchen furniture are creating ranges which do not look out of place in a living room context and some are even supplying non-kitchen furniture such as room dividers, dining tables and chairs and occasional seating to match.

The noticeable increase in the popularity of both matt and glossy lacquer finishes and the swing away from dark oak in traditional designs towards other gentler hardwoods, means that there is now much greater freedom available to designers in planning colour schemes for mixed-use rooms. It has always been possible to have furniture designed and made for such situations, but the fact that it can now be bought from many makers' standard ranges makes this type of kitchen a more economical option.

The main space economies arise from the lack of walls, not to mention the doors through those walls and the space they take up when opening. You are also unlikely to need two tables, one in the kitchen area and another to eat elsewhere.

It is possible to have a super-compact kitchen which quite literally disappears into a cupboard when not in use, though this is hardly a realistic option in a family house. However, allocating one corner or part of a wall to a kitchen area which disappears behind doors or a curtain when not in use would be ideal in a bedsitter, so long as laundering and utilities' storage could be handled in the bathroom.

Far left: Your first reaction to this room will probably be to ask where the kitchen is. Yet if you throw an oilcloth cover over the table to convert it into a working area, this becomes a totally practical dual-purpose room. Note how the contents of the shelves to the left have been positioned to keep those used most often closest to hand.

Left: This no-nonsense layout puts practicality before all else, with the possible exception of the bare brick walls. The dark marble tops are eminently stain-resistant and the choice of equipment and fittings was dictated by the functional needs of a keen cook who frequently entertains. Both of these room settings illustrate how you can create functional cooking-eating areas in quite small spaces without spending lots of money and at the same time achieve a warm and inviting atmosphere for the others who will no doubt share the room.

THE BARE NECESSITIES

Above: The space occupied by this kitchen area connects the sitting and dining areas of a small apartment with a tiny walled garden. No attempt has been made to disguise the working area, even though cupboards hide all the storage. The use of stainless steel permits the sink to be moulded into the top surface and the waterfall edging helps to prevent water spilling onto the parquet floor. The chrome taps and stainless steel hob merge well into this setting.

Right: The table base forms a visual link with the kitchen area and the repeated use of shades of white gives the whole space a feeling of airiness. Cantilevering the sink base out of the wall reduces its apparent bulk. It would form more of a visual block if the cupboard continued to the floor in the usual way. Note the small Scholtes oven and grill, which also contains a roasting spit, below the hob. The refrigerator is housed in a tall cupboard opposite the sink.

The problem faced by most people is the creation of a comprehensive kitchen in a space which is too small, the wrong shape or awkward for some other reason. Yet there are many people who, because of their lifestyle, would not want a large kitchen even if they had the space. In such cases the problem is to reduce the kitchen to its bare essentials. Working surfaces, equipment and storage for foods, kitchenwares and utensils still need to be practical, but the scale of the problem is quite different.

In the past this sort of kitchen often took the form of a nasty little box, hidden away somewhere out of sight, hot, noisy and unpleasant to work in. Now, however, even those who live alone are more likely to be keen on cooking and may even entertain regularly. So the solution is to create a kitchen where you can work while enjoying the company of others in the adjoining area or simply get a meal for yourself without the risk of missing your favourite TV programme.

Much space can be saved by using small-scale equipment, as shown here. In this type of kitchen it makes good sense for just about everything to disappear behind doors when not in use, and, as cooking will be concentrated in such a small space and wear and tear will be even greater than usual, the choice of fittings and surfaces must be superpractical, durable and easy to keep clean. Granite, Corian or stainless steel are the best options for surfaces, with the choice dictated by the visual character of the adjoining living area.

Lighting needs to be planned with special care, and consideration will have to be given to waste disposal. The best solution in this instance is the combination of a waste disposer for food scraps and a rubbish compactor for boxes, tins and non-returnable bottles.

Whereas in a family house you should go to any lengths to avoid creating a kitchen in which a frequently-used pathway cuts across your main working area, in a one-person apartment, for example, it is worth thinking about passageways, lobbies and other odd corners as possible sites. As you are probably the only person there most of the time, the usual problems and dangers that would be inherent in trying to cook in such situations simply don't arise.

Even a space 6 ft (1800 mm) wide is capable of accommodating a working area on one side and a set of shelves or a tall, shallow cupboard on the other. With less space than this, it may be possible to squeeze a sink into a corner and cook entirely on plug-in equipment plus a wall-mounted microwave oven.

The versatility of modern system kitchen furniture is such that requirements like this can usually be dealt with without resort to specially-made joinery. Alternatively, it may be worth considering furniture which was designed for other uses, such as bedrooms or sitting rooms. With ingenuity, this can be adapted to suit both the visual and practical needs of the area you have planned.

If the kitchen area has to be right in the sitting room, rather than adjoining it, there are two possible ways to make it disappear when not in use (if you want it to, that is). One is to arrange everything so that large cupboard doors can be swung out to uncover everything when you are cooking and then swung back again when you have finished. If you adopt this idea, try to arrange the design in such a way that large doors do not have to be continually opened and closed to reach different areas of storage during food preparation. The other possibility is to have a drop-down cover which acts as a splashback behind working areas when they are in use but covers them at other times. Taps can be wall-mounted, instead of set conventionally in the sink rim or worktop, with the spout swung out of the way when the sink is covered.

Yet another possibility is to set the sink and a ceramic hob below the level of the surrounding surface and then cover them with pieces of the same material when you are not cooking or clearing away. This idea works particularly well with a hardwood top, which can easily be disguised as a table area or sideboard when you want a sitting room rather than a kitchen.

MAKING THE BEST OF IT

Where kitchens are concerned, necessity is often the mother of ingenuity. The kitchen on this page had to be created on a landing because it was in a house that had a dining- and sitting-room off to the right, bedrooms above, and a utility room and garage below. The kitchen opposite had to be created in a rented room, which meant that legally any permanent fixtures became the landlord's property. What was needed was a kitchen that could be moved when the tenancy expired.

The owners of the landing were able to choose kitchen furniture that, by repeating the tones of the structural timbers, merges into the fabric of the building itself. Even the plate rack seems an organic element. The open-shelf storage immediately above the staircase is potentially dangerous, but is used for items rarely required. Only adults live in the house, so there is no risk of a child running from the sitting-room to the stairs just as a pot is being lifted from the hob across to the sink.

An interesting touch is the way in which use has been made of the alcove into which the sink is fitted. The width of the staircase below means that the alcove is some 3 ft (900 mm) deep. By using the whole of this depth for the working surface, extra space is created for the storage of small items used often when working at the sink.

Even the fact that the landing has an unusually high ceiling has been put to use, with fresh produce stored in hanging baskets alongside the house plants. This is probably a better way to store vegetables and fruit than that used in most orthodox kitchens.

The bachelor kitchen in the rented room was bought as a self-contained kitchen package, completely housed in a free-standing cupboard. All that is needed is a pair of power points, a cold water connection and a drain. When the owner moves, he or she takes it with them, together with the folding dining furniture, the woven rug, the curtains and the light fitting.

Maximum use of space has enabled the users of this kitchen-on-a-landing to achieve an acceptable level of efficiency. In the foreground can be seen some of the pans hung on racks above the hob. The wall rack for knives is an excellent idea in any kitchen and the fact that the alcove into which the sink has been fitted is some 3 ft (900 mm) deep is a storage bonus. The only real lack is drawers on the sink side of the kitchen, but a cutlery basket is a perfectly acceptable substitute and lets you carry cutlery settings easily to the table.

The one-piece stainless steel top in this take-it-with-you kitchen contains a two-ring electric hob and an integral sink. Hot water is fed directly from the small storage heater above the sink. This particular package has a refrigerator rather than an oven, but options from different makers provide a wide range of choices. The package is a neater solution to one-room living than trying to fit plug-in equipment around furniture and equipment supplied by a landlord.

THE UNFITTED KITCHEN

Since World War II, most new thinking about kitchen design has been based on the concept of a fitted kitchen, involving cupboards which are fixed into place. Historically, this is a relatively novel idea. If we look back over the centuries most kitchens (if they were furnished at all, apart from a few shelves and hanging racks) contained a couple of dressers, a table and at a later date a sink in one corner.

Domestic kitchens only started to be "fitted out" about a century ago and even as recently as the 1920s and 1930s in most homes people stored their food and utensils in an all-purpose kitchen cabinet which they probably took with them when they moved.

The earliest fitted kitchen units needed to be fixed to a wall because most were too flimsy to stand alone, but it was really the adoption of wall cupboards as standard items in almost every "modern" kitchen which convinced people that all kitchens should be "fitted". That word is now taking on a wider meaning, with designers as concerned with fitting the kitchen to the needs of the family using it as with making the furniture fit the space available. Also, kitchen units have now evolved to the point that the best must be regarded as good quality furniture and they certainly no longer need a wall to support them.

The trend in kitchen furniture design has now moved a long way from simply filling the space available with plastic-lined cabinets fitted with doors of more or less elaborate design. Furniture-makers now vie with each other to create new practical storage details and this book is packed with the evidence of a new concern with function and aesthetics.

It has been noticeable that in the last few years people refurbishing their kitchens have shown increasing interest in using traditional furniture, either antique pieces or reproductions of old dressers, tables and other items. However, when space is at a premium, fitted furniture has the advantage that you can ensure that every inch available is used.

Sooner or later one of the design leaders in the market was bound to create a new type of furniture which, while it could be ordered specifically to fit the space available and offered all the mod cons of the best unitary systems, nevertheless comes as free-standing units which do not have to be fixed in place. In fact several companies have thought of this idea at about the same time but the first fully-fledged system to be offered generally is Contempi by Leicht, which was the sensation of the 1986 International Furniture Fair at Cologne in Germany.

The thinking behind the Contempi design is to concentrate storage between hip and shoulder height but, within that zone, to make everything as accessible as possible. In fact the key to the Contempi design is the complete abandonment of the wall unit and the adoption of pull-out storage, shallow open shelves, drawers or cupboards with glass doors for every other situation.

A Contempi kitchen is organized into work zones (see pages 154–157), each featuring surfaces of the most suitable materials. The furniture has also been designed with specific items of equipment in mind, so as to take advantage of the space-saving and practical benefits of the new generation of ovens, hobs and sinks.

Although the Contempi concept can be applied to almost every kitchen, except perhaps tiny spaces, it will probably work best in cases where the kitchen has to share a room with a dining, living and perhaps also a sleeping area. The technology used means that all the practical problems normally involved in such situations have been overcome, and the range of styles available in the furniture elements is compatible with current thinking on interior design and colour.

The latest developments in cooking, food storage, dishwashing and ventilation equipment mean that a kitchen can now be an attractive and relaxing family room. Some kitchen furniture is now so attractive that it is increasingly common for kitchens and dining areas to share the same space, but up until now there has been no escaping the fact that the kitchen area has looked like a kitchen area.

Now Contempi has bridged the practical and visual gap, grasping the opportunity offered by the latest technology to solve some of the spatial problems of modern urban living. No doubt many other makers will follow with their own versions of the basic concept but Leicht have ensured that the idea of the kitchen as the centre of the home will take on a whole new meaning for many people.

The brilliant new
Contempi concept by
Leicht is likely to be one
of the most influential
designs of the 1980's. It
consists of a series of
complete kitchen com-
ponents, some of them
containing ready-fitted
hobs or sinks, which you
fit together to suit your
requirements and the
space available. Costs
are potentially lower be-
cause professional fitting
skills will not be required
in most cases. Contempi
follows current thinking
on the design of compact
kitchens by considering
the layout as a series of
workzones which need to
be related in a logical
order.

1 Cooker hood
2 Wall racks
3 Cooking zone
4 Wall storage drop-down
board
5 Food preparation area
6 Sink area
7 Tall store or appliance
housing

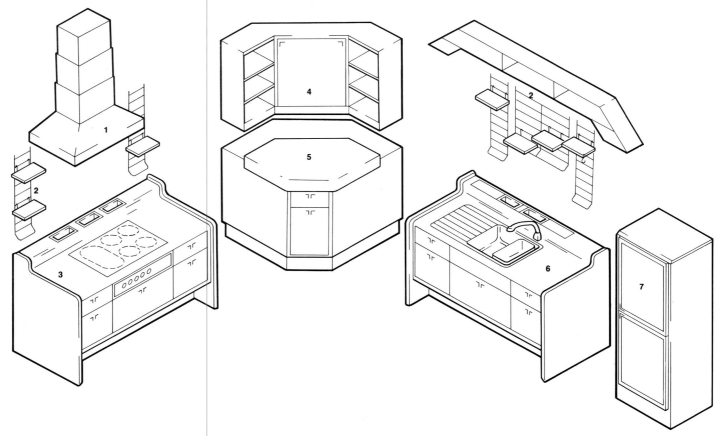

CHECKLIST DESIGN 1

What is your kitchen for?

The main reason why kitchens vary so much is not that people have different tastes in furniture or food or even that the rooms concerned are different shapes and sizes. It is that we all have slightly different ideas about the role of the kitchen in our lives and what we expect to do in it. That is why looking through books and magazines to find illustrations of possible layouts and colour schemes can be so frustrating. The examples you will see were designed to meet particular requirements and the chances that these were the same as yours are very small.

Practically all experienced kitchen designers approach their work in a similar way, asking their customers lots of questions about what their kitchen will be used for; how many people will use it; what will be cooked in it and what other tasks have to be handled there; whether they have any special requirements or hobby interests which call for space in the kitchen, not to mention pets, play areas and so on. There is no point in looking at the space you have to work in until it can be viewed with a realistic understanding of what has to take place there.

The mistake most people make in planning their own kitchens is to start off by considering what might be fitted into the space. Quite apart from the fact that small kitchens cannot be planned satisfactorily on a grid which does not take account of storage or working facilities at different levels, if you tackle the job this way your ideas about the layout tend to be influenced by the limits of what appears to be possible.

Instead it is better to set down all your requirements in a logical order first and not to think about the space you have to work in until you have a clear idea of what you are trying to achieve and what your priorities are. Every kitchen involves compromises. Only by ensuring that you thoroughly understand your own requirements can you make certain that the new design is created to fit your personal needs, whether the final design is yours or someone else's. Otherwise the design will probably be a hotchpotch of new and old ideas, perhaps visually attractive but unrelated to your practical objectives.

The best designs are the result of close co-operation between the customer and an experienced designer. The role of that designer is to suggest

Many current ideas on small kitchen design are incorporated in this Bulthaup kitchen: a peninsula, full use of the midway space between worktops and wall cupboards, and a variety of different storage systems to suit items of different shapes and sizes.

alternatives, explain the consequences of different solutions and put all the final choices together into a workable concept which can be created within the budget limits you have set. Giving a designer, however experienced and skilled, a free hand is not a wise decision. He or she will have lots of new ideas to suggest to you but the best designs always result from an interplay of ideas, requirements and counter-proposals between designer and client.

The next few pages are devoted to a checklist of questions that need to be asked during the planning of almost any kitchen. You may well think of others as the list of questions is potentially inexhaustible, but at least those that follow will provide you with a framework within which to create your own specification.

Do you cook only in the kitchen?

It is quite common to cook or finish off dishes away from your main cooking area. You may have a secondary cooking area in a breakfast bar or dining zone. Some dishes can be cooked entirely of finished off in your dining room, or you may wish your microwave cooker to be sufficiently portable to use near a garden barbecue or perhaps in your living room during parties. In this last instance, it might be a good idea to incorporate the microwave cooker in

a wheeled trolley, so that it can be used wherever necessary. However, in a small kitchen the trolley will require a planned position where it is accessible for use but out of the way.

You may need to allow space for a heated trolley or heated trays if food is often eaten some way from the kitchen, either during formal dining or perhaps as TV meals. It is better to plan specifically for such requirements than to provide general purpose storage and hope to fit in everything once the kitchen has been completed.

Will you be laundering in the kitchen?

It is worth going to considerable lengths to avoid laundering in a small kitchen because washing machines are inevitably noisy and sorting soiled clothes is not the most hygienic use for worktops. The bathroom may be an alternative site, or if you are really short of space perhaps a laundry cupboard, housing both the washer, dryer and related storage, could be fitted under a staircase or elsewhere with a carefully sound-insulated door.

If you have to launder in the kitchen, remember that the latest fully-integrated washers and dryers (not to mention the combined washer/dryers discussed on page 34) are much quieter than simple free-standing machines. The smaller the kitchen, the greater the problem you will have with noise and you may well decide that the extra cost of these quieter machines is justified for that reason.

Where do you store house-cleaning equipment and materials?

If the answer is in the kitchen you will save lots of space by planning a properly-fitted utility cupboard. In almost all cases a deep cupboard between 12 in. (300 mm) and 18 in. (450 mm) wide will house all your equipment and materials so long as it has adjustable shelves, racks for polishes and aerosols and fittings for your vacuum cleaner tools. An unfitted cupboard would need to be twice this size and will quickly become a mess.

Do you have storage space outside the kitchen?

Do you keep a freezer in your garage or do you have a cellar or separate utility room? If so, what should be stored there and what should be kept in the kitchen readily to hand?

Ideally all kitchen-related storage would be in the kitchen itself, though a cool cellar for vegetables in bulk, bottles and backup stocks of dried goods is a desirable exception. However, if you want a really big freezer, site it elsewhere if you can, to reduce noise and heat in the kitchen, with a smaller frozen food section handy in your fridge.

If you often bulk-buy on monthly trips instead of shopping week by week and you simply cannot create more storage space in the kitchen, consider storing backup stocks in a cupboard or even a loft space elsewhere. But first look at how you are using space in the kitchen above wall cupboards, in corners and below base units. Most kitchens contain lots of space which can be put to better use with a little thought.

Some small or awkwardly-shaped kitchens will be in large buildings, and sometimes it will not be possible to enlarge them. In such cases it may be practical to use space elsewhere for laundering, utilities, storing bulk dry goods, housing a deep freeze or even storing rarely-used china or utensils.

If you cannot house your chest freezer in a garage or outhouse, consider using the loft space so long as there is easy access and a large enough trap door to get it up there. It may be easier and less costly to alter the access to your loft, incorporating roll-down steps, than to make major changes to your kitchen or to buy a new upright freezer.

Try to find a space somewhere to create a utility cupboard outside the kitchen, behind a door, under a staircase or even on a landing. Such a cupboard does not need to be deep, and from the accessibility viewpoint two shallow cupboards (with storage racks on the backs of the door) will be much better than one deep cupboard.

How many people will use the kitchen area?

How many regularly work together on main meal preparation or perhaps come there simply to get snacks? How many join you there for coffee and a chat, to read the paper, do their homework, play or simply keep you company? If you breakfast or take family meals in the kitchen, how many people need to be seated at a time? Would they mind sitting on stools (which take up less space) or must you allow for normal dining chairs? Must the seats be stored in the kitchen area or can they be brought into the room at mealtimes?

How many people do you entertain for formal meals?

This question helps to establish how much serving space is required in the kitchen because, whether you serve straight onto plates, into dishes or onto trays, you will want to aim for a clear space of 12 inches square (300 × 300 mm) by your hob or cooker for every person at the table.

Is your kitchen also a play area?

Young children generally wish to keep close visual and verbal contact but they are quite happy to have their own "territory" to play in. A breakfasting corner or even the further side of a peninsula or table may be the perfect solution, but it is as well to plan some cupboard space in the kitchen exclusively for their toys.

How about pets?

People tend to have strong views about pets in the kitchen, one way or the other. However, if you are going to share your cooking area with a cat, dog, bird or other animal, it is better to plan space for them (and their food) than leave it to chance.

Do you have hobbies or interests which call for space in the kitchen?

A sewing corner is a common requirement, but the fact that you grow a lot of your own vegetables or have bagfuls of fish or game to prepare for the freezer from time to time will also call for special facilities, if only a big sink. Home wine-making and an interest in Eastern or Oriental cookery must all be regarded as activities for which special provision should be made. A cool larder is an essential for home-made wine or beer and excellent ventilation is a must when cooking curries. A Chinese wok poses particular problems, as there are few normal hobs on which it will work satisfactorily.

What is your normal weekly meal preparation pattern?

How many times a day do you prepare cooked meals? Should cooking facilities be split to enable one person to work on the main meal while another is getting a snack or dealing with certain special items? Only by listing the amount of use you make of your cooking equipment can you establish how extensive the facilities need to be, how many ovens, hobs and specialized built-in or plug-in appliances you require.

Once you have listed your notes on these and the questions in the following pages, common sense will be enough to enable you to work out the design solutions. Planning kitchens is basically a practical business, where an ounce of common sense is worth a pound of quasi-science. A professional designer will show you interesting ways to meet the practical requirements you have listed and should also be able to "package" the total kitchen more stylishly, but your better understanding of your needs will be a vital factor in the final design.

CHECKLIST DESIGN 2

How would you describe the kitchen you want?

Write down as many words as you can think of to describe the sort of atmosphere and visual effect you are trying to create. Use words like "comfortable" or "formal", "inviting" or "dramatic" rather than attempting to be more specific at this stage. No designer will thank you for setting firm stylistic limits right at the beginning and one way to ensure that you get a boring kitchen is to take a catalogue picture or refer to a complete display and say: "Make that fit my kitchen."

Should the emphasis be on the working or the living aspects of the room? Much kitchen furniture now available would have been thought more suitable for a living room 20 years ago and there is a growing awareness that a strong sense of style is not incompatible with the kitchen as a practical working area.

What role should colour play in the room?

Colours can be used in a background sense to create mood or can become features of the design in their own right. Generally speaking, strong colours will make the room feel more active, either as a working area or for living in. Primary colours in particular add drama to the design, especially when they are used as colour co-ordinates. For example, if the basic colour is white and bright red is used repeatedly for accessories, handles, jar lids and other fittings, the effect will be very striking. Mixed primary colours can be used successfully to brighten up a basic design, but they should be used with great care in all but the smallest areas.

Remember though that colour is subject to fashion, and the stronger the role it plays in the room the faster it will "date". It can be argued that if the design is well executed it should still be attractive even when the fashion from which it derived is over, but in practice the kitchen is not often a room that can be retained exactly as originally designed for long. New accessories, utensils and equipment are added over the months and years and these will tend to break down carefully co-ordinated colour schemes.

How soon do you need the new kitchen and how long must it survive?

If your new kitchen has to be designed and fitted in

How much design and money it is worth putting into your kitchen depends on how long you intend to use it. If you plan to move home in a couple of years, opt for a simple, inexpensive kitchen like this.

the time between signing a contract for the purchase of a new home and moving in, the choices open to you will be severely limited. There is no better way to ensure that your kitchen will be unsatisfactory in the long run than to rush the process of choosing, ordering and fitting out.

Much depends on how many years service you expect from the new kitchen. If the answer is that you will probably be moving again in a couple of years, an "instant" design made up of readily-available furniture, equipment and fittings will probably be quite adequate. If on the other hand this is to be your retirement home, you will be making decisions which must still hold good in perhaps 30 or 40 years' time.

Few people realize that almost everything manufactured for use in the kitchen has a planned working life in satisfactory order. Standards vary considerably but, to take one example, the standard that applies to most furniture fitted by builders in

new estate house developments in Britain calls for a satisfactory working life of no more than seven years.

In choosing equipment, furniture, working surfaces, floorings and all the other items which go to make up a kitchen you need to have a clear idea of how long you expect them to continue functioning satisfactorily. Make your requirements on this clear to any supplier involved, otherwise your chances of obtaining redress if the goods do not meet your needs are very small.

Again, it is a matter of common sense in most cases. If you want things to last a long time, avoid plastics and most forms of composite construction, shiny surfaces and paintwork in high-wear areas. Ask if any finishes with which you are not familiar can be repaired or retouched if damaged or worn and if in doubt get the answer in writing.

Kitchens which are designed for a long or perhaps indefinite life will incorporate a large number of natural and traditional materials. It is no accident that those really old kitchens which still survive are made of a limited range of softwoods, hardwoods, stones and other materials. Many others have been used at different times in the past, especially in the relatively recent past, but few have survived.

Factory-made system furniture is not designed to be serviced like a car, with parts renewed as they wear out. If drawer runners, hinges or worktops reach the end of their useful life, you probably face total replacement. Refitting a kitchen is inevitably a major expense and, once you have retired or settled into your final family house, the chances are that the need for further expenditure in ten or 15 years' time partly or entirely to replace worn-out worktops or furniture would pose a serious problem. You will probably have to accept that certain items of equipment, such as dishwashers or laundering machines and perhaps cookers, may have to be renewed in due course. Even the best fridges and freezers will probably not last for much more than 20 years if you want to minimize future expenditure on your kitchen, the only precautions you can take are not to use equipment of non-standard sizes, to avoid re-using old machines which are bound to need replacing fairly soon, and to avoid buying system furniture with a limited life expectation.

On the other hand, if you are planning to move again within five years you have three choices: opt for furniture and equipment which is not built-in and can move with you; spend more on equipment to take with you and as little as possible on the furniture, so you can throw that away with a clear conscience; have the best possible kitchen you can afford, enjoy it for the next few years and hope that the residual cost will be reflected in the price of the house when you sell it.

Should the kitchen be modern or traditional or don't you mind?

All this talk of styles, materials and finishes implies that we all care a great deal about what our kitchens look like, but the fact is that many people don't, so long as they are comfortable and work well. Many people would refuse the gift of a designer-planned, fitted kitchen, and an increasing number are opting for rooms furnished at least partly with antiques or furniture adapted from previous uses.

Choosing modern furniture probably implies factory-made units to most people but that need not be the case. Much of the best built-in furniture is now so expensive that tailor-making may be a realistic alternative financially. In practice, at some levels of the market the lines between system furniture and tailor-made are becoming blurred, because the range of factory-made options is now so great that they amount to manufacturing to order.

On the other hand not all tailor-made furniture is of superior quality. The fact that cupboards are designed in attractive styles or with spectacular finishes does not mean that, at a functional level, the value behind the doors matches the price charged. Many people are now opting for a traditional style for their kitchens, probably because this is linked in their minds with their perception of lasting quality. Yet that arose more from the materials used and methods of construction than from the look, so simply buying solid wood doors for your plastic or chipboard cupboards will not of itself make them last any longer.

There is also a distinction between a kitchen that is traditional in layout, with a big central working table, larder, dressers for pans and chinaware and at least one big china sink, and one that is fitted with modern furniture with traditional cupboard fronts and details. In a small kitchen there will not be space for a truly traditional kitchen layout, though in a combined kitchen-dining room the old layout approach is often still the best.

Most really old kitchens were in fact very simply

A permanent home – perhaps one in which you intend to retire – calls for durable furniture and equipment. In *this solid wood kitchen the only things that will eventually need replacing are the ovens and fridges.*

furnished, mainly because every surface had to be easily washable owing to the appalling ventilation standards in 17th-, 18th- and 19th-century homes. The visual atmosphere in such kitchens arose mainly from the contents of the dresser shelves and the foods and utensils hanging around the room from racks, hooks and rails. Many of today's "traditional" kitchens, with their wealth of elaborate furniture, hand-painted finishes and added non-functional detail, are entirely spurious, although they can be a delight to look at and make very pleasant centres for family living.

Will the kitchen be designed up to a standard or down to a budget?

The fact that more activity has to be concentrated into less space means that small kitchens have to withstand more wear and tear, relative to their size, than larger spaces. Worktops are used more inten-

sively, cupboards opened and closed more often, drawers used more frequently and so on.

In theory, as the smaller the space the less furniture and equipment you can fit into it, this should be balanced by the ability to spend more on individual items. In reality however the very reason why your kitchen is small may mean that you are having to tailor the desing to fit a strict budget.

Here are a few suggestions therefore to help you get the best possible value for your money.

Working surfaces
Insist on the very best, probably hardwood, stone or Corian, or perhaps a combination of these. The less worktop you have the harder it has to work and nothing creates a greater sense of discomfort in a small kitchen than scratched or burned worktops.

Sinks
Get the biggest you can fit in because a small sink will start to show its age very quickly. Also, the bigger the sink the less water tends to spread around the kitchen. Use a second bowl as a part-time draining area for the same reason.

Cupboards
Use open shelves for storage in as many cases as possible. The hinges on cheap cupboard doors usually fail quickly, sometimes in only two or three years, and in the case of more expensive cabinets the door may account for more than half of the cost. Related to what you can store in it, a fully-fitted larder is the best value-for-money storage space in your kitchen.

Equipment
Think carefully before buying a bargain-offer cooker. In most cases your money will be better spent on an all-plug-in set made up of a table-top cooker, microwave, toaster, electric pans and a sandwich-maker. Don't opt for cheap built-in cooking equipment. If the money runs out, it is better to buy really good appliances over a period of time. They will be safer, pleasanter to use, cheaper to run, easier to clean and last many years longer.

If you have to save costs, cut down what you spend on cupboards and put the money into working surfaces and equipment. Buy the best built-in equipment you can afford and if necessary buy it one piece at a time, using plug-in appliances as a stop-gap.

CHECKLIST DESIGN 3

What should the design theme be?

Now that the kitchen is a family room again in most homes, it is as important to consider the decoration and atmosphere as it is to ensure that the room functions well as a workshop. Often it is just one feature of a room which sets the character or acts as a focal point visually, creating a sense of individuality or perhaps a theme for the overall design.

Sometimes features are introduced, but quite often in small kitchens some aspect of the room or the fittings and equipment force you to approach the design in a certain way. If this is the case in your kitchen, if perhaps a low or sloping ceiling, awkward door positions, projections or alcoves spoil the shape of the room, try to make a positive feature of them by incorporating them into the design. Emphasize them even, and repeat the shape or pattern in other ways until it appears to have been part of your design choice.

This is an approach to design that is particularly relevant in small kitchens because it is usually easier to hide awkward details in larger rooms. For example, if one section of a ceiling slopes sharply, because of a sloping roof above or the intrusion of a staircase, pick up the same angle in the decoration with diagonals in the paintwork, by sloping the lay of tiling or even painting a diagonal pattern on the furniture. Or, to take another case, if the proportions of a window are unusual, repeat the same proportions in the styling or layout of cupboard doors or shelves.

In creating new kitchen layouts in an older house, the height of windowsills may be too low to align with normal worktop height. Consider setting a lower surface in this position, perhaps to eat at or for use as a low-level working surface. Alternatively, if there has to be a worktop at this point, create an indoor window box, as this often makes an excellent position in which to revive houseplants or establish a small herb garden. Don't forget to fit a lip at the back of the worktop to prevent things from falling over the edge into the plants.

Sometimes a small kitchen area is created by partitioning off part of a much larger room and as a result the ceiling may be disproportionately high. Don't be tempted to fit a lower false ceiling as this will almost certainly make the resulting space feel claustrophobic. Painting the ceiling a dark colour to make it appear lower is not a good idea either for the same reason. Simply paint the ceiling white and

By sacrificing wall storage and opting for the stark constrast between dark grey and white, the designer of this kitchen achieved a clear, uncluttered style that is unmistakably modern.

bounce light off it to provide the background illumination for the room as a whole. The ceiling will then simply disappear.

You should also resist the temptation to fit cupboards right up to the ceiling, unless you are still desperate for storage space after using every other inch including the plinth area. Instead, consider suspending light fittings, racks or other fixtures on chains or wires at suitable points. You might even consider fitting a rack which pulls up out of the way into the space above when the contents (perhaps pans or large utensils, dried flowers, garlic or strings of onions) are not required.

If you have a problem with pipes or other relatively small projections running up a wall on which you wish to store things, cover the offending item completely and then to one or both sides build shelves of roughly the same depth in order to disguise the underlying problem. Corner soil drains from a bathroom above are best disguised by fitting a diagonal panel across the corner, or better still, use this as a position in your room plan for a larder, cooking hob or sink set across the angle which will enable you to lose the pipe quite easily. Having

created such a corner void, make use of it as a route for other services such as heating or water pipes and electrical cables.

How can I create design features?

Focal points can be created in a design by making a feature of something which is a necessity in the design anyway. For example, an eating corner might be fitted out with high-back settle benches and perhaps a corner glazed cabinet to display some special chinaware. You might decide that an inset pastry slab should be of spectacular pink, green or brown marble instead of the usual white. It won't show the inevitable stains so much and stays just as cool in practice.

If you have an unusual collection of cooking utensils, pans or kitchen knives that are visually attractive in their own right, are in regular use and therefore get cleaned in the normal course of events, hanging them in a group on the wall can be a practical move as well as creating an interesting focal point.

The smaller the kitchen, the more unobtrusive the furniture itself should be. If you want to introduce splashes of visual drama, do it with brightly or subtly-toned accessories, storage containers or perhaps a feature panel in tiling. Another interesting possibility is to use a neutral overall tone in the furnishings and decor and then introduce stronger colours or textures in such details as light baffles, cornice rails, wall racks or even handles.

Finally, though the trend in modern fitted kitchens is to hide the equipment as best you can, there is something in the counter argument that much of it is now so attractive that items should be bought or refinished in bright colours. One way to integrate older equipment into a new setting is to have all the appliances, new and old, re-enamelled to a common finish which may either tone in or contrast with your overall decorative scheme.

How do I design a spectacular kitchen?

Improvements in kitchen ventilation systems, better understanding of lighting and the enormous range of finishes, colours and designs now available for furnishings, furniture and kitchen equipment all mean that you can approach the room with the specific intention of creating a setting which is spectacular and yet totally practical from the working viewpoint. There is no reason to confine yourself to a dramatic colour scheme or some special finishes on the furniture. Consider also creating exciting shapes in the layout itself – patterns of equipment set in the furniture, unusual working surface shapes or sculptural arrangements of shelving and cupboards.

It is noticeable that some of the leading Italian furniture-makers, such as Snaidero/Abaco and Schiffini and the German trend-setters like Bulthaup, Poggenpohl, SieMatic and Allmilmö are now incorporating dramatic styles in their current ranges. Metals such as brass and brushed steel are being reintroduced and it is now commonplace to find various types of granite being used for entire kitchen worktops.

Central working islands, peninsulas of irregular shape, large canopies above cooking hobs and elaborate glazing designs for display cabinets are just some of the design ideas that are now becoming commonplace in real kitchens, rather than merely features of shops' displays or advertising photographs. Perhaps buyers are becoming braver but also many people have now lived with two or three fitted kitchen designs and are beginning to realize that practical working areas can be visually exciting as well.

There is increasing interest in ever more detailed re-creations of traditional kitchen settings which are by no means confined to large-scale layouts copying the design of the classic Victorian backstairs room. French companies in particular have shown how special details like plastered or bricked arches and canopies and a host of other period Provençal features can be integrated very successfully into quite small areas to give atmosphere combined with practicality.

All of these ideas are worth considering when a kitchen area has to be created in a room which is also used for dining or which may even be the main living room as well. Careful planning of the essential services, aided by the range of special equipment now available, makes it easier than ever before to create combined designs like this successfully. Those items in the kitchen which have tended to look unavoidably utilitarian in the past, such as sinks and cooking hobs, can now either be arranged so that they disappear when not in use or can be made of materials which are attractive in their own right, for instance, coloured enamelled steel and tinted ceramics.

Shape and form are essential elements of design. Blocks of storage and an ingenious pull-out table that is round rather than rectangular determine the visual appeal of this kitchen in which colour plays a secondary role.

The traditional approach, involving no more than a walk-in larder, a dresser, a big sink, a cooking zone and a table or mixing surface can actually be fitted into a remarkably small area with care and ingenuity. The trend has moved away from designing a kitchen and then adding fancy details simply for decorative purposes and towards using attractive colour finishes, interesting materials and textures and dramatic but practical elements in the layout scheme. However you approach the design, boring kitchens are now a thing of the past, or should be if full advantage is taken of all the new and exciting components currently available.

Will an attractive kitchen cost me more?

The immediate answer is "no" but that has to be qualified by adding that attaining a better visual mix may require additional time and trouble. Much will depend on how the job is being handled. If you are tackling the design yourself, a critical factor will be the amount of care and planning you are prepared to invest. Many people make the mistake of thinking they can achieve good results without going

through the proper stages of design that a professional would. Take the trouble to draw out the layout and elevations (see page 160) and then colour these in or put together a collage of the materials that you intend to use. You would not expect a professional designer to achieve satisfactory results without doing this so why think you can manage successfully without following the same painstaking but essential procedure.

Relatively few people who plan kitchens professionally are actually trained designers. In Britain this is largely because there is no generally accepted course or qualification in kitchen design. You will therefore have to judge a designer's proposals on their merits but it is worth remembering that you are unlikely to get really excellent results from companies who cannot put together a proper colour presentation for you. The market is very competitive indeed so this is one case in which it really does pay to shop around for expertise combined with value for money.

CHECKLIST DESIGN 4

How much cooking do you do each week?

We probably all consider the amount of cooking that we do each week as "normal" but this is one case where the range of what constitutes normality is considerable. Alternative "packages" of cooking equipment suited to different needs are illustrated on pages 22–23, but first you must recognize exactly what your needs are and how these can be related to the types of equipment now available.

Just as important as how much and how often you cook are the questions of how many people are likely to be involved in cooking at the same time and what they may wish to do. Certain types of cooking involve the use of far more equipment than others; a simple comparison being between reheating a pre-cooked meal from the freezer and preparing a traditional Eastern meal with a large number of side dishes.

How often do you cook?

How many times a day do you usually prepare a cooked meal? Do you often have cooked breakfasts, and if so, can you manage with simple plug-in facilities or will you be using your main oven and hob? If you have the space to store the equipment concerned, it can pay to use snack-makers, sandwich-toasters and other such specialized gadgets for cooking individual items rather than heat up a main oven. This is less true of the latest hot-air and multi-function ovens, which rarely need pre-heating and have remarkably low running costs, but even so there is less involved in cleaning a snack-maker than cleaning an oven.

How many people cook in your kitchen?

It is now commonplace for virtually every member of a family to get involved in some aspect of cooking and the chances are that at some time during the week they will all wish to do so at the same time. Clashes will only be avoided if it is possible for one or two people to work at the hob at the same time, while a third is using the main oven and perhaps a fourth preparing a snack in the microwave or under the grill.

Not only does this situation affect your choice of equipment but also means that space should be created around each item for preparation and serving. Although it may be more expensive to buy a number of separate pieces of cooking equipment and install them in different parts of the kitchen than to have one large multi-purpose cooker, you need to consider your priorities. Is it more important to save money on this important aspect of equipping the kitchen or should you decide instead that, if economies are necessary, they should be made on other items?

If the number of occasions on which you cook more than once a day or have to share the facilities with others are limited, it may be that this requirement can be ignored. Do think about how things may change in the future, though. If you have small children now and the chances are that you will still be living in the same house when they are teenagers, remember that the trend is for more people to get involved in more of the cooking more of the time. It will be much less costly to plan for that requirement now than to make alterations when the time comes.

How elaborate are the meals you cook?

Even if one person does practically all the cooking in your kitchen, most major meals involve cooking several items at once. It may therefore be more convenient to separate your hob, your oven and your grill or secondary oven so that each becomes the centre of a minature work zone. In a small kitchen this is unlikely to increase significantly the amount of walking about that you have to do, but having a small preparation and serving space by each item of cooking equipment will certainly make each cooking operation that much easier.

For instance, mounting a microwave oven on the wall above a working surface clears that surface for working and serving. If the cooker is also capable of conventional roasting, baking and grilling, its usefulness will be much increased. Although it is quite practical to cook several items at the same time in a modern hot-air oven, this facility is only useful if they can all be cooked at the same temperature. When you need to roast or bake two things at the same time at different temperatures, you will require two ovens and a practical solution is to combine a hot-air oven with either a microwave or grill.

Some double ovens offer a microwave cooking facility in the second compartment but this is rarely combined with a true roasting or baking capability. The problem is that, with microwave cooking alone

If the space is available, a kitchen can be designed to provide both a main and a secondary cooking area. In this kitchen the main area (above) contains a preparation area, a gas hob, a double oven and a toaster and coffee-making machine.

in the second "oven", it may be difficult to find somewhere to heat plates or serving dishes. It is therefore worth considering a quite separate though smaller secondary oven.

The standard types of gas and electric hobs usually have four cooking positions. You may well find that there are occasions when you need more and many makers of ceramic electric hobs now offer models with a fifth zone for simmering or warming only and in most cases one of the cooking zones is adaptable for pans of different shapes and sizes. This last facility can be very important in a ceramic hob, because you should never use pans which do not entirely cover the ring in use. If you are using a large casserole or fish kettle, the enlarged heating area offered on some hobs will also ensure that your pan is heated more evenly.

One of the difficulties inherent in electric ceramic hobs is that, if you spill something while cooking, the fact that the surface is completely flat means that the spill is likely to spread. This may be

The secondary area of the same kitchen is devoted to the preparation of light meals and snacks. The oven is a microwave. There is enough space in this area (an L off the main kitchen) for a small dining table.

especially disastrous if you are cooking something containing sugar because, if the sugar cools before you wipe it up, sugar crystals may fuse with the ceramic surface and create a permanent rough area which cannot be repaired. Some of the latest types of hob, which incorporate a halogen "cook by light" element, offer an automatic facility which can be pre-set to bring a pan to the boil and then switch to a simmer setting.

If you regularly need more than four or five hob cooking positions, it is quite possible to create a hob layout to meet your requirements perfectly by combining modular elements. These are offered by many makers in ranges covering gas rings, orthodox electric or ceramic plates, deep-fryers, electric griddles and large oblong plates for giant pans. Most ranges also include stainless steel heatproof resting plates and some even offer a matching miniature sink, which can be a bonus if your hobs are set into a central island or peninsula some way from the main sink.

What sort of pans will you be cooking with?

Most people choose their pans to suit the type of hob or cooker they have selected and in the case of a ceramic electric hob it is vital to do so if it is to work satisfactorily. However, some recipes and cooking methods you use may involve special types of pans, such as a Chinese wok for stir-frying or the many types of flameproof terracotta or stoneware used in traditional Italian and French cookery. In these cases you may well have to choose the hob to suit the pans.

The only way to heat a wok satisfactorily is to use a very high-output gas ring. As you also need quite a large space around the burner, the best solution is to choose a two-burner hob and set this slightly apart from your other hob positions. As stir-frying is an "instant" cooking method, the two-burner hob could be placed in a central table or peninsula at which you also sit for meals, where it may be useful for fondues and other table-top cooking.

How many do you cook for?

This question is aimed at establishing the size of pans you are likely to use, especially for roasting and baking, and how much space will need to be provided around your oven and hob for serving. Even though you may only seat three or four in the kitchen itself for breakfast or light family meals, it is important to think about how many people you entertain at family gatherings or dinner parties, particularly if these are regular events.

If you only rarely cook for large numbers, you may not require a full-size main oven at all. It may be both cheaper and more economical in space to buy two smaller ovens, one combining microwave with hot-air roasting and baking and the other microwave with radiant roasting, baking and grilling.

Even if your cookery is quite elaborate small-scale equipment can be adequate if the quantities involved are small. A small kitchen can function effectively if it is equipped with a small microwave cooker, a portable plug-in hot-air oven, a two-burner gas hob set in the centre of a peninsula working-eating area, a toaster, kettle and plug-in slow-cooker. This setup is more than adequate for daily cooking for two yet also copes easily with three-course dinners for six or eight and the occasional larger party.

Such equipment cannot cope with roasting a 20 lb (10 kg) turkey, but is it worth spending money (and using vital space) on fitting larger equipment for a once-a-year requirement? Consider settling for a 12 lb (6 kg) turkey instead and use the money to create more working space and storage to suit your personal requirements.

It is very important to avoid a situation in which you keep cramming cooking equipment into a small space but neglect to allow an adequate amount of space around each item for working and serving. If you have to compromise, it is better to have less equipment with enough space around it to ensure that it can be used with maximum efficiency.

In any case, many of our ideas about how much equipment we need are based on experience of working with cookers which are hopelessly out of date by today's standards. Even a small wall-mounted microwave oven has more sheer cooking capacity than two or even three rings on a normal hob. So if you have space problems, do remember that you are better off with two small ovens than one large one and that today's multifunction ovens can handle more cooking in less space and time, at less cost (and with far less cleaning afterwards) than the monsters of a decade ago.

How big a sink do you need?

The answer to this question depends less on whether or not you have a dishwasher than on what you use the sink for. Even if you have a dishwasher, it is unlikely that you would use it to clean oven shelves for example and, unless you have a pyrolitic self-cleaning oven, there will be times when these need soaking for some time rather than a quick wash down.

You may not previously have thought of a sink as a piece of equipment, but the latest system sinks certainly deserve to be considered in this way. They incorporate fitted accessory drainers and racks, chopping boards, colanders and strainers and lift-out secondary bowls, so that you adapt them to the task or tasks in hand.

The advantage of multi-bowl system sinks and their accessories is that they enable you to carry out a number of tasks at more or less the same time and to adapt the sink areas to changing needs. You can have lots of clear soaking space for oven shelves or divide the space up for rinsing cups while someone is preparing vegetables, yet still have somewhere to pour water off a saucepan or strain off some pasta. In other words, opt for the largest sink you have room for but ensure that it comes with accessories to turn it into a sink-and-drainer or two or three smaller working areas.

Think about which bowl should contain the waste disposer if you have two separate bowls, or whether you will have two bins below the sink instead, one for compost waste and the other for bottles, cartons and tins. Alternatively, consider a waste bin that is large enough to take an entire dustbin liner, and set this below a trapdoor in your worktop which might take the form of a lift-out chopping board of hardwood or knife-proof plastic.

Another space-saving possibility is to use a mechanical waste compactor for part or all of your kitchen rubbish. This electrically-powered machine takes up very little space (about the same as a medium-size built-in waste bin), yet will contain large quantities of compressed rubbish, sealed up in a moisture-proof bag. It sounds alarming the first time you hear a large bottle being reduced to a handful of shards but it is a reliable, clean and normally trouble-free machine.

Will your new dishwasher take your dinner service?

There used to be a great difference between the size, shape and layout of the basket shelves in alternative brands of dishwashers, but with the adoption of international standards for place settings the difference is now diminishing. However, it is still well worth taking some of your china to check sizes and numbers if the dishwasher you favour is an unusual shape or size, as some models and makes are far more adaptable than others.

The better machines now available can be set to wash the most delicate overglaze-decorated china and lead crystal glassware without the slightest risk of damage. If you doubt this, lend your supplier a spare or damaged item to test over a period of weeks in his demonstration dishwasher before confirming the delivery. The secret lies in very careful temperature control and selecting a machine with a wash action that is energetic rather than violent.

A dishwasher with cold-fill only will almost certainly give you better all-round results, partly be-

Waste disposal is made easier with a built-in waste bin. The wooden lid can be used as a chopping board: it lifts out so that waste can be pushed into the bin. The knife rack in the background combines safety with accessibility.

cause very high temperatures are no longer regarded as the secret of the best wash quality, but also because sudden changes in water temperature cause more problems than the range of temperatures used.

Do you have to launder in the kitchen?

If you have to launder in a small kitchen, it may be difficult to find space for a conventional dryer and even more difficult to duct out all the hot wet air it produces. The second problem is being solved by several manufacturers, who now offer condenser dryers in which all the moisture from the wet washing is collected in a plastic container or flushed down a handy drain, while the air is simply reheated and recirculated. This process is much cheaper and no ducting is required at all.

The first problem has been solved for most families by the latest generation of combined washer-dryers. Because it takes twice as much drum space to dry any item as it does to wash it, most washer-dryers can only dry approximately half their full potential wash load. However, they are so

cheap to run on half-load settings for washing that it pays to wash smaller loads more often. This completely overcomes the problem of having half-loads of wet laundry hanging around waiting for dryer space and may even mean that you need to allow less space for storing dirty laundry while waiting to build up a satisfactory load. As most of these combination machines use the ductless drying system and require cold water only for washing, they are very simple to connect and install.

How much fridge and freezer space do you need?

If you require a really large freezer it is better to site it outside the kitchen if you possibly can and have a smaller frozen food section in a multi-zone refrigerator for open packets, meal portions and bulk ice. If you wish to freeze food which you have prepared yourself, however, ensure that this frozen food section has a four-star rating or the food quality will not be satisfactory when defrosted.

The trend in refrigerators is now strongly towards multi-zone designs with a variety of self-contained compartments for special purposes and

dispensers for cold water or drinks and ice cubes as well. Even more important is the fact that many large refrigerators now contain a chiller area in which dairy products, vegetables and fruit can be kept cool and fresh, rather than over-refrigerated at the lower temperatures required for safe storage of meat, fish and cooked foods.

The best refrigerators have now become efficient, multi-purpose foodstores which are adaptable to a wide range of requirements at different times of the year. If a refrigerator is combined with a larder, which may also be used to house dried and tinned foods, the other cupboards and storage in the kitchen can be devoted exclusively to kitchenwares, pans, utensils and china. In a small kitchen the key to creating a workable layout is to choose a big multi-zone fridge, a large multi-purpose larder and a large but adaptable sink.

First of a new generation of extractor cooker hoods, this model by Gaggenau is powerful, quiet and all but invisible. There is still plenty of useful storage space in front of the compact motor unit.

CHANGING THE WAY SPACE IS USED

If your kitchen area, however small, is well-designed, has all the facilities you are likely to require, and you are happy working in it, consider carefully before making alterations or expanding.

In most houses and apartments, you will have a fixed amount of space within which to redesign or refurbish your kitchen, but this isn't always the case. Quite often the space you have at present has resulted from decisions taken many years ago about where the kitchen should be sited, and you may well feel that the decision taken then does not suit you now.

As a major kitchen refurbishment is probably the most complex interior job you are likely to undertake, this may be the best possible time to reconsider how space is allocated within your home. For instance, it might well fit your family lifestyle better if the kitchen were moved to a different position in the house or combined with another room to create a larger shared space. In some cases, it may be possible to extend the existing house, either to create an entirely new area for the kitchen, or to enable you to rethink which rooms in the house are used for what purpose.

In the case of apartments, or houses which have been divided up to form apartments, you will often find that the kitchen now occupies a much

smaller area than it did originally. A space may have been created for it by partitioning off part of a larger room or the original kitchen may have been altered into a dining room, with the kitchen shifted to what was originally a scullery or utility area.

One solution is to knock out the partition and combine the two spaces to form a larger area which can be used for both cooking and dining. Now that the kitchen is a family room again in most households, this solution can work very well. Technically speaking, this will probably not be a major building job because the wall you will need to remove is unlikely to be load-bearing and the changes needed to services and drainage should be relatively minor.

Solving the kitchen space problem by changing round the way in which existing rooms are used can be technically difficult, especially if water, gas, power and drains have to be run to an area where they have not been required before. However, if the benefits are great enough it will be well worth the trouble involved. It may also be a long job but you will probably be able to continue using your old kitchen till the new one is completely ready.

It is worth considering moving the kitchen to a different position in older houses which have been extended several times over a period of years. During the first half of this century it was general practice to relegate the kitchen to the back of the house, with the result that, after several alterations, the kitchen is now not only too small in relation to the size of the house but also badly placed, away from the heart of things.

The only solution may be to draw up a complete ground plan of the house and look at how each area relates to the others and what improvements are possible. You might discover that, after trying several alternatives, a new layout is possible which returns the kitchen to a more central position in the house, yet does not involve major structural changes or radical alterations to the services and drainage system.

Extending a house to create more room for a kitchen should always be regarded as a last resort. However, in some cases it is the only practical solution, and if this is so, beware of the tendency to make such an extension larger than it needs to be. As the ideal size for a kitchen is approximately 12 ft square (3.5 m square), not allowing for an eating area, and it is unlikely that the existing kitchen is less than half this size, at least in theory no ex-

tension for kitchen use alone should need to be more than roughly 60 sq. ft (6 sq. m).

The point to keep in mind is that extensions should be in scale with the original house, unless you are considering an architect-designed major enlargement. You should also consider carefully the new relationships between the spaces within the house once the extension is complete and the kitchen installed in it.

The other danger with creating an extension for a kitchen is that, if the cost of the extension is too great, it may leave you an inadequate sum to spend on the kitchen itself. If you are working on a tight budget, you will almost certainly do better to enlist expert help in designing and fitting a really top-class kitchen in the existing space (taking advantage of the best equipment, furnishings and fittings to get the most out of what space there is) rather than commit yourself to an extension and then have to fill the resulting enlarged space on a shoestring budget.

More space does not, of itself, mean a kitchen that is better to work or to live in. In fact, once you have lived in a really well-designed small kitchen, the chances are that you will not want to move away from it. Though in an ideal situation you might choose a kitchen of the dimensions mentioned above, many excellent, compact and very efficient designs are created in spaces of 10 ft square (3 m square) or even less. However, to do this you will need to plan every aspect of the equipment and more especially the storage, down to the last inch or centimetre.

If adding more space to the house is the only viable option, instead of moving the kitchen into the new area created consider using this as a dining or garden room. One interesting possibility, if you don't want to extend at two levels to create a bathroom or bedroom above as well, is to add a conservatory instead of a "solid" extension. With modern double glazing techniques, such rooms can be totally practical right through the year, even in northerly areas and they do tend to look more acceptable as an addition to a house than many of the home extensions one sees.

There is absolutely no reason, even in a house shared with teenagers, why the kitchen should not be sited in a living room. In fact, in some cases this will enable you to create two living areas where previously one might have been used exclusively as a dining room or kitchen plus breakfast room. And if you *are* sharing a house with teenagers, the chance to have *two* living rooms is too good to miss.

Elsewhere in the book we have shown several examples of kitchens occupying one end or one corner of a much larger room. This can work very well in a family situation and in any case fits in with the way in which most of us live today. Good ventilation and care in choosing quiet equipment can mean that the working aspects of the room need not be too intrusive.

Quite often a kitchen appears to be too small, not so much because of an actual shortage of space but because doors and windows are in the wrong places to allow the space to be used effectively. It may therefore be worthwhile altering poor positions or window sizes and that could be a lot less costly than combining rooms, adding an extension or having furniture tailor-made to fit awkward spaces.

In older houses you will also often find that windows are inconveniently low in relation to the normal height of a worktop, so that it may appear impossible to position a working area in that part of a room. One solution would be to alter the window but another is to make the working area in that position deeper than standard, so that the worktop is 30 in. (750 mm) deep or more, then fit an upstand at the back to prevent things falling off. The well created can be used as a place to revive houseplants or grow fresh herbs.

If windows in such a situation are too large, consider fitting open shelves across them. China can be stored on such shelves or even glass storage jars so long as they contain things which will not be damaged by continuous daylight. Or this could be a site for plants. Space the shelves so that they obscure no more than half of the window area, however, or the effect created will appear too cluttered.

One of the problems which can arise when moving a kitchen into a living area is that existing heating radiators are sited where you wish to place cupboards. One answer to this problem is to fit a "kick space" fan convector (see page 46) but it is quite possible to set base cupboards in front of a radiator. Set the cupboard forward so that there is a gap of at least two inches (50 mm) between the back of it and the face of the radiator, and have the working surface made oversize so that it covers both the cupboard and the space at the back. Then fit a grille in the face of the plinth and another at

the back of the worktop, so that cool air can enter at the base of the cupboard and leave through the top grille again.

The heat from a radiator placed in such a position is unlikely to damage factory-made cupboards but if yours are of solid wood construction it may be worth lining the backs with reflective foil, facing towards the radiator.

The most difficult problems which arise when moving a kitchen from one part of the house to another concern water supplies, waste pipes and electrical wiring. If the floors in the area concerned are of wood construction it is likely that there will be space within them for all the necessary pipes. Even if the floors are of concrete it will probably not be difficult to create a channel for services, provided you are on the ground floor.

However, if your kitchen is to be at a higher level in the building and you have a solid floor, a little more ingenuity may be called for. It is normally possible for most pipes and cables to be hidden in a working void between the cupboards and a wall (see page 47) but sometimes they will have to be run in a direction which makes this impractical. The worst case of all is when water pipes and a drain have to cross an open floor. The solution is to set the kitchen up on a platform six or seven inches high (150–175 mm).

Make this higher area as large as possible and ensure, for safety reasons, that the step down to the level of the remainder of the room is well away from the main working areas. The space created between the real and the false floor should be adequate to provide for the "fall" required by a drainpipe over quite a long distance. Insulate such pipes very thoroughly or they may produce unpleasant gurgling noises just beneath your feet when the dishwasher empties.

An attractive idea in such a "two-level" kitchen area is breakfast bar extensions from the worktop, overhanging the lower floor of the rest of the room. Because of the additional height of the bar you will need to sit on extra-tall stools and also fit a foot-rail to the back of the counter.

One thing worth remembering is that there is absolutely no reason why a kitchen has to look like a kitchen, especially when not in use. Kitchen units can be disguised as sideboards (with covers over the sink and hob when you are eating or relaxing). They can be hidden in cupboards or behind curtains or blinds.

If your requirements are satisfied by the minimum of facilities, it is worth considering something along the lines of a bedroom vanity unit, but with a kitchen sink set into a cupboard with storage above and a fridge below. A microwave cooker and small hob can then be fitted into a wheeled trolley. This can be used near the sink for meal preparation and pulled into the living area for hot snacks.

In all of the cases discussed so far the aim has been to increase the amount of space allocated to the kitchen or to combine it with another area. This is not always the requirement however, and you may wish to separate off the kitchen area completely by dividing an existing room. There is normally no need to build a proper wall or even a framed partition in such cases because the kitchen furniture itself will probably be strong enough structurally to form the division.

Such an approach obviously makes it easy to create a hatchway for serving into the adjoining area at mealtimes. Some makers offer partitioning and dining furniture to match their kitchen unit ranges, so that a complete, enclosed kitchen area can actually be ordered from one company.

PLANNING FOR SAFETY

Safety is not something you add to a kitchen like extra cooking utensils. A safe kitchen is one that was designed properly in the first place, observing rules that will make it a less dangerous place in which to work. Kitchens contain items which can poison, maim, cut, burn and cause all kinds of problems ranging from broken nails to chronic backache. When designing a new kitchen therefore, ensure that as many of the hazards as possible are eliminated, or at least neutralized.

Here a typical kitchen layout is shown, with many of the safety points noted that need to be observed at the design stage, plus details which could make every kitchen safer if they were adopted.

1 Choose a double sink which is large but not deep. If you work regularly at a sink which is more than 7 in. (170 mm) deep, you will probably suffer backache even if the top into which the sink is set is at the correct level for your height (see note 11). Having two sinks means that you always have a bowl available for rinsing things in clean water.

2 Ensure that you only use taps which meet local standards for drinking water supplies. In Britain this means the National Water Council (NWC) Standards. Using taps which do not meet these standards may mean that you will drink water from a foul roof tank rather than fresh from the main.

3 Store regularly-used china as close to your sink and dishwasher as possible. If it is stacked on shelves, ensure these are easy to reach without bending or stretching, and that plates and saucers are not stacked more than six high.

4 Use a kick-plate to open the door to your waste bin so that you have both hands available for heavy pans. Use a bin which closes automatically when the door shuts.

5 Place electrical sockets at a height at which they can be reached over the equipment plugged into them and right where they will be needed. Then shorten the leads of all plug-in electrical gadgets to ensure there are no loose loops of cable.

6 Buy a full range of top-quality kitchen knives and try to keep one for each type of meat, or at least one for slicing cold meats. Keep your knives really sharp because you are much more likely to cut yourself on a knife which is not sharp enough. Don't put sharp knives in drawers with other utensils. Use a knife block or better still a wall rack which enables you to identify knives easily.

7 Use all the space you can immediately above your worktops to keep chopping blocks, utensils, spices and other frequently-used items readily to hand, minimizing reaching, bending and twisting.

8 The safest possible hob arrangement sets the rings along the rear half of the worktop, leaving space in front for preparation and serving, and at the same time eliminating the risk of knocking a pan off one of the rings. Small children cannot see, let alone reach, pans in such a position.

With one exception, there is little comparative information about the relative safety of different types of cooking hobs. The exception is the coiled element electric ring which has been shown consistently in home accident and fire statistics to be the largest single cause of kitchen fires. The reason is that, when working at full output, such rings reach a temperature, about the flashpoint of oil (at which it will burn rather than just smoulder), which is high enough to set light instantly to many commonplace kitchen items that may drop accidentally onto the ring. The habit of hanging cloths above a working hob to dry out is a common cause of such fires. Gas hobs would also seem to be a danger in this way, yet by comparison they hardly figure in the fire statistics. The great danger with gas hobs is lack of proper permanent ventilation. Some form of permanent fresh air input to the room is essential if you are cooking by gas. Otherwise, a burner set low or a pilot light could be blown out when a door to the room is closed suddenly, causing a risk of explosion unless your hob is fitted with the latest flame failure safety devices. Finally, there should be a worktop of at least 12 in. (300 mm) on each side of a hob or cooker and preferably 18 in. (450 mm).

9 The only truly safe cooker hoods are extractors incorporating a fat removal filter. Recirculating hoods do not remove water vapour from the kitchen, nor the fumes from any pan fire which occurs in your absence, and they often become clogged with fat and are then a fire hazard in their own right. Simple extractor fans should not be set immediately above a hob as they will certainly become clogged with fat in this position. The surface of a cooker hood should be at least 30 in. (750 mm) above an electrical hob or grill and 32 in. (800 mm) above a gas hob or grill.

10 Hinged doors to base and wall cupboards should ideally be no wider than 18 in. (450 mm) and certainly no wider than 20 in. (500 mm). Wider wall cupboard doors can cause injuries if left open.

11 Your main sink worktop should be about 6 in. (150 mm) below the elbow height of the main user.

12 Try to arrange for a second working height for hob cooking, chopping and pastry-making at about 4–5 in. (100–125 mm) below your main worktop height.

If you have small children in the family, keep all poisonous liquids such as bleaches, powerful cleaners and solvents in a cupboard fitted with childproof catches.

Other common causes of accidents in kitchens are slippery floors and climbing on chairs or stools to reach items from high shelves or cupboards. Shiny or glazed floorings, which become slippery if a mixture of oil and water is spilled on them, are inherently less safe than terracotta tiles, textured vinyl tiles such as Amtico, cork sheet or tiles, and planked wood finished with a non-slip sealer. If you have shelves or cupboards which are beyond easy reach, make sure there is a proper set of strong steps kept permanently in the kitchen. The plinth-stored steps shown on page 58 are ideal but a step-stool makes a good alternative.

If an accident should happen

Cuts and burns are the most common type of kitchen accident, and as the kitchen is also the most likely place for accidents in the home, it is the best place to keep your emergency medical kit. All chemists sell ready-packed kits to enable you to give first aid for virtually any minor accident. Fires are the other problem, and most of these arise when a pan containing oil or fat catches alight on the hob. By far the best way to deal with them is with a fire blanket which can be bought from most hardware stores, pre-packed in a protective tube. Fire prevention experts advise that this blanket should be stored where it is visible and easily accessible, not far from the nearest exit door. Do not keep it out of sight in a drawer, or immediately adjacent to the hob. Don't ever pour water on a pan fire of any sort or attempt to remove the pan from the hob. If you do not have a fire blanket, turn off the hob and smother the flames with a lid large enough to cover them, or with a damp cloth or towel, the larger and heavier the better. Then leave the kitchen, closing the door behind you. Call the fire brigade even if you think you have put out the fire. It could re-ignite, and in any case you may well need an official fire report for insurance purposes. Take no chances – leave the building if there is the slightest risk of the fire spreading.

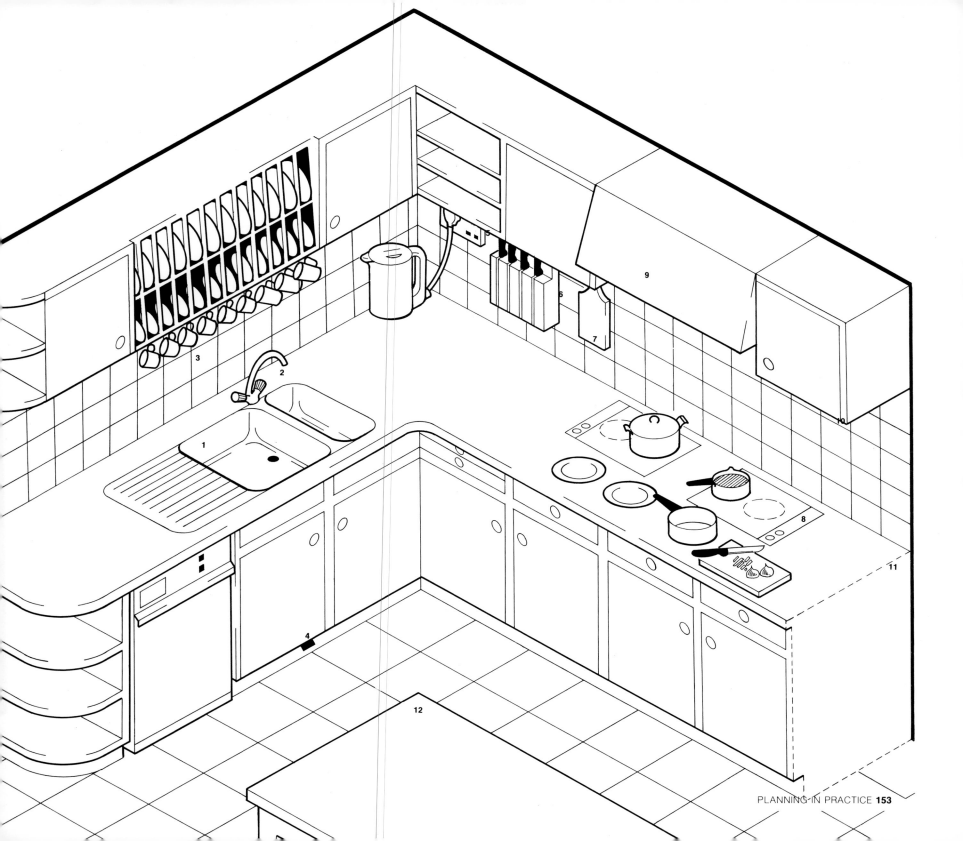

PLANNING KEY AREAS 1

Every kitchen is made up of a series of working and living zones, and the ideal way to approach any particular layout is to plan each of your zones and then arrange them within the space available to the best advantage. If all kitchens could be designed by planning the perfect layout for your personal requirements and then fitting the walls round the space you need, the job would be simple. Unfortunately, most kitchen spaces are smaller than this ideal calls for, are awkward in shape or have doors or windows in the wrong places or some other structural problem requiring compromise.

Whatever the space you have, the key work zones still exist in some form. Ignoring the need to make some allowance for washing up or serving a meal won't make the requirement disappear. It will simply make the job concerned more difficult to do.

The primary work zones in every kitchen are for: food preparation and dishwashing; food mixing (including the oven); and cooking (including the hob). Then there are secondary zones which may need to be related to the first three to some extent. These are for: serving; food storage (refrigerated, fresh and dry goods); eating; relaxation and play.

The primary work zones must contain the main equipment and utensils used there and storage space for them. The approach to kitchen design set out in this book is based on the idea that food storage should be concentrated, either in a large fridge, a larder or dry-goods store as appropriate, instead of split up between a large number of smaller non-specialized cupboards. It is for this reason that food storage is considered as a zone in its own right, rather than allowing for it in each of the primary work zones. The result is that these zones can be much more compact than would be the case otherwise and food storage in total also occupies a more limited space.

There is an optimum size for each work zone, depending to some extent on the volume as well as the type of work to be done in it. Planning each zone in this way as a self-contained work area also means that one person can work in each without clashing with others working elsewhere. As the normal pattern of shared use in a kitchen is for people to tackle different tasks instead of sharing the same job, this approach works well in family kitchens, even if the total space involved is quite small.

The food preparation and washing up zone

Tasks performed in the zone
The preparation of fresh foods and those that need cleaning; dishwashing, including the disposal of table waste; the cleansing of kitchenwares and utensils.

Equipment
Sink or sinks (two are preferred, so that water and waste can always be disposed of during another task); taps; dishwasher (optional); waste bin or bins (two are increasingly preferred); waste disposer (optional).

Working surface
Minimum of 24 in. (600 mm) required each side of sink. One side may take the form of a drainer, so long as it is flat enough to double as a working area. Suitable materials are granite, maple, teak, iroko, Corian, stainless steel and plastic laminates.

Related storage
Kitchen crockery: Most-used crockery should be stored in a rack or on narrow shelves within the midway area; alternatively on the lowest shelves in a wall cupboard.

Table crockery: In a china store close to, but outside, the main work zone.

Colander, strainers and large sink utensils: In pull-out storage within the zone, ideally between the sink and cooking zone.

Cook's knives: In a wall-mounted or worktop knife block, which should also be within easy reach of the mixing zone.

Peelers, small utensils: In a shallow, divided drawer immediately beside the sink and ideally near the cooking zone.

Kitchen cutlery: In a shallow, divided drawer, or can be stored in the eating or serving zone.

Plastic bags, foil, paper towels and clingfilm: In drawers, or box drawers that can be pulled out and taken to other areas, or on wall racks.

Tea and hand towels in current use: On rails near a heat source if possible. Damp towels should never be kept behind a closed cupboard door. Heated kitchen towel rails are available.

Washing-up materials and utensils; "wet" cleaning materials (bucket, floor cloth, etc.): As many as possible on door-back racks below the sink. Ideally keep "wet" cleaning materials out of the kitchen in a utility or laundry room, otherwise use a pull-out base tray to simplify access.

Waste bin/bins: As near the sink as possible, either mounted on the back of a door or in a pull-out base tray, or reached through a lift-out lid or cutting block in the worktop. It is now commonplace to have two bins, one for food scraps and the other for tins, cartons and non-returnable bottles. One way to reduce the volume of your weekly waste is to use a waste compactor (see page 36).

Chopping boards: On the wall or in the slide-in space below the sink.

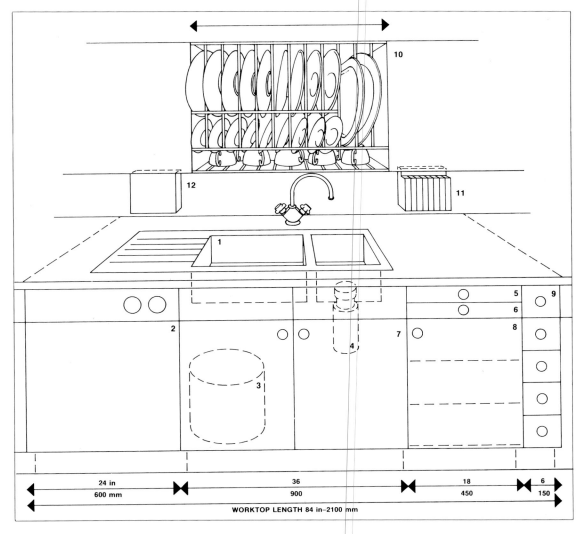

1 Double sink
2 Dishwasher
3 Waste bin on door
4 Waste disposer
5 Small utensils
6 Kitchen cutlery
7 Cleaning materials
8 Large utensils on pull-out shelves
9 Paper towels, clingfilm,
foil etc
10 Kitchen crockery in wall
rack
11 Kitchen knives in wall-
mounted block
12 Cutting board hung on wall

24 in	36	18	6
600 mm	900	450	150

WORKTOP LENGTH 84 in–2100 mm

The food mixing zone

This is probably the most variable working zone in any kitchen because its size, layout, equipment and furnishings will need to be planned to suit personal requirements. This zone is now becoming increasingly important, as there is definitely a trend towards more elaborate home cookery and less use of convenience and prepared foods. If, however, you buy a high proportion of your meals ready-made at the supermarket, it may be worth considering combining this area with the serving zone and incorporating your microwave oven in it.

The layout of the mixing zone will also depend on whether you have chosen a built-in oven and separate hob or opted for a combined cooker. The arguments in favour of split-level cooking, even in the smallest kitchen, are discussed elsewhere, but it is worth mentioning here that, if you choose a combined cooker, it is inevitable that the mixing, cooking and serving zones will all overlap and that the kitchen will be more difficult to work in as a result.

This last problem will be multiplied if more than one person wishes to use the cooking facilities at the same time. Each piece of cooking equipment should be associated with its own working area, however small. Using the available space in this way will enable a number of different cooking tasks to take place at the same time without serious clashes.

Tasks performed in the zone
Food mixing; dry food preparation processes associated with roasting and baking (as distinct from the wet preparation and cleansing at the sink); the handling of roast and baked foods during cookery.

Equipment
Oven or ovens; the microwave cooker may be in this zone or in the serving zone, depending on its role in your kitchen; if you have chosen a separate wall-mounted grill, it may be sited in this zone or the cooking zone, depending on convenience and the way you work; mixing equipment, which should ideally be sited in such a way that it can be permanently plugged in and no more than 1 ft (300 mm) from the position in which it is normally used; kitchen scales; other plug-in equipment used in mixing and preparation.

Working surface
The optimum area is probably 3 ft (900 mm), but it should be at least 2 ft (600 mm) and rarely needs to be more than 4 ft (1200 mm). This is an area which benefits from a deeper than standard top, say 30 in. (750 mm), as the back is often used as a place to keep mixing equipment and large storage containers. Suitable materials are light marble or granite, Corian, maple, stainless steel and plastic laminate (though this requires protection from hot pans).

Related storage:
Utensils: In divided drawers of suitable depth; fittings and accessories for food-mixing equipment should be stored in compartmented drawers. Alternatively utensils can be kept on a wall rack and mixer fittings in a specialized midway unit (see page 60) or worktop wall cupboard with roller shutter door (see page 61).
Pastry board, cooling rack, trivets: Boards, ideally ranging from small to large, should be as accessible as possible, perhaps wall-hung or stored on edge in a cupboard. Racks and other flat pastry-making accessories are best stored on edge in a cupboard.
Mixing bowls: In a pull-out drawer or basket.
Roasting and baking tins and sheets: On edge in a vertically-divided cupboard, above the oven, or in a drawer below the oven, though they are then less accessible. This space is best used for casseroles and big pans.
Foods (flour, sugar, dried fruits, herbs and spices): The decision on the extent to which these should be stored within the zone or in a larder or dry-goods store will depend on how often you bake and roast and how accessible the larder or store would be. Small items should be stored on small shelves, in door-back racks or in specialized midway units.

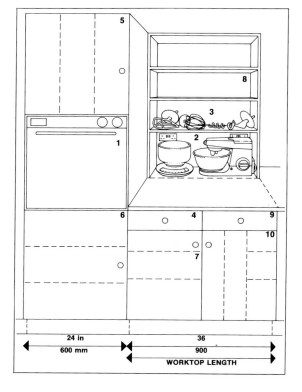

1 Built-in oven
2 Equipment store
3 Mixing utensils
4 Utensils in divided drawer
5 Baking trays and trivets, stacked vertically
6 Roasting tins and casseroles
7 Mixing bowls on pull-out shelves
8 Baking and roasting materials; dried foods
9 Herbs and spices in divided drawer
10 Pastry boards, trivets, rolling pins and large utensils

The cooking zone

There is a trend now for the cooking areas to be split, with some dishes being dealt with at or near the table or in a secondary cooking zone, which may be centred on a breakfast bar or peninsula. With the adoption of split-level cooking, the main cooking zone is increasingly set in a surface which divides the primary kitchen area from the rest of the room. The latest flush-inset ceramic hobs even enable you to set a hob in a table surface, with a cloth thrown over it at meal times. However, the same rules apply for planning your main cooking zone wherever it fits into the overall kitchen layout.

Tasks performed in the zone
Boiling; steaming; frying; griddling; grilling if a wall-mounted grill is set in this zone.

Equipment
The main hob or hobs; secondary built-in hob for special purposes (griddling, deep-frying, etc.), if required and not in secondary cooking or eating area; wall grill if required and not in the mixing zone; plug-in cooking equipment; combined microwave/baking oven/grill; cooker hood or extractor canopy.

Working surface
Absolute minimum of 1 ft (300 mm) each side of the hob and ideally 2 ft (600 mm) each side. If a microwave is sited in this zone a further clear area of at least 18 in. (450 mm) should be allowed for work associated with this, though the space below can be used if the microwave is wall-mounted. Suitable materials are granite, maple and stainless steel. Corian and plastic laminates can be used but require protection from hot pans.

Related storage
Small utensils: In a divided drawer below the hob or in a container on the worktop or on a rack in the midway area.
Pots, pans and casseroles: In deep pan drawers, on wall-hanging racks or in a tall, shallow-shelved pan-store cupboard.
Plug-in equipment: On the back of the worktop or in a tall, shallow-shelved pan-store cupboard.
Seasonings: If not in the mixing area, on a wall shelf or door-back rack.

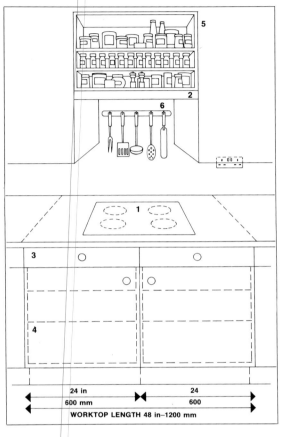

1 Cooking hob
2 Concealed extractor hood
3 Divided utensil drawers
4 Internal basket drawers for spoons
5 Condiments and seasonings on narrow shelves
6 Rack for serving utensils

The serving zone

This only needs to be a small area but it makes all the difference to any kitchen to have a space allocated to minor tasks, such as making breakfast or a snack, toast and coffee or assembling dishes for a major meal which will then be taken through to the dining room. If this space is not allowed for, these jobs have to be carried out in the food mixing or cooking zones even though other work is often already in progress there. In very small kitchens the serving zone is commonly combined with the eating zone, and as the chances are that only snacks will be eaten there, this can make good sense.

Tasks performed in the zone

Assembly of the elements of meals to be taken elsewhere; snack-making; tea- and coffee-making; preparing non-cooked breakfasts.

Equipment

The refrigerator should be in or near this zone, ideally set between this and the mixing zone; kettle; coffee-maker; microwave, if not kept elsewhere, ideally wall-mounted; this could be the area in which secondary cooking equipment is sited (for example a warming cabinet or hotplate); toaster; various other plug-in appliances such as a sandwich-maker.

Working surface

Minimum of 18 in. (450 mm), though 3 ft (900 mm) or even 4 ft (1200 mm) would not be excessive if you entertain frequently or have a large family. Suitable materials are maple, Corian, tiles and plastic laminates.

Related storage

Chinaware and cutlery: The serving zone is an excellent place to keep everyday chinaware, especially breakfast cups or mugs, soup and cereal bowls and plates. Store them on shallow, closely-spaced shelves, an open rack, a low shelf in a wall cupboard or worktop wall cupboard (see page 61) or in a dresser. Store cutlery in jars or baskets on the worktop or in a shallow, divided drawer.

Breakfast cereals, jams, sauces, herbs and spices: These may be kept in a cupboard in this area instead of in the larder or dry foodstore.

Bread: In an airtight container at room temperature or in a special bread drawer, where you can also keep the breadboard and bread knife.

Serving utensils and everyday table cutlery: In a shallow drawer below the worktop if it adjoins the cooking zone.

Trays: In a vertical slot between cupboards or inside a cupboard.

Table mats and linen: In a drawer below or beside the cutlery drawer.

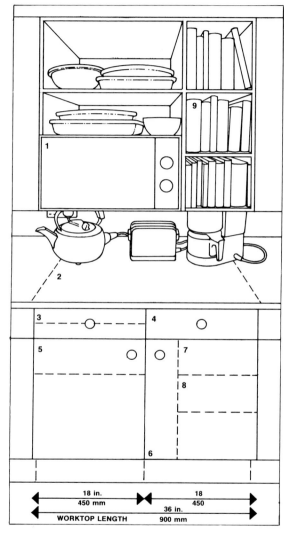

18 in.
450 mm

18
450

36 in.
900 mm

WORKTOP LENGTH

1 Wall-mounted microwave oven
2 Kettle, toaster, coffee-maker, etc
3 Serving utensils and cutlery
4 Table linen and mats
5 Breakfast foods
6 Trays
7 Internal bread drawer
8 Microwave ovenware
9 Cookery books and large serving dishes

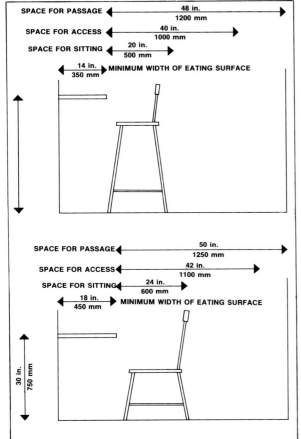

SPACE FOR PASSAGE · 48 in. / 1200 mm

SPACE FOR ACCESS · 40 in. / 1000 mm

SPACE FOR SITTING · 20 in. / 500 mm

14 in. / 350 mm · MINIMUM WIDTH OF EATING SURFACE

SPACE FOR PASSAGE · 50 in. / 1250 mm

SPACE FOR ACCESS · 42 in. / 1100 mm

SPACE FOR SITTING · 24 in. / 600 mm

18 in. / 450 mm · MINIMUM WIDTH OF EATING SURFACE

30 in. / 750 mm

The eating zone

As a family room, the kitchen must include a place where meals can be eaten, and many kitchens that were adequate for use by one person for meal preparation and dishwashing are inadequate for this wider role. This is often the reason for enlarging the kitchen area by combining it with the dining or even the living area in an open-plan arrangement. If, however, you wish to eat in the kitchen and there is space to do so, there are some dimensional requirements to keep in mind.

It takes less space to seat someone on a high stool than on a chair but you may of course prefer to eat at normal table height. More space needs to be provided around the table if anyone is to pass behind the seated person. The diagrams (left) show the space required by each person seated for a meal in the kitchen area and how much space needs to be provided for circulation behind them. You may decide that you do not wish to create a fixed eating area, but instead use one of the many pull-out or swing-down table systems that are now available. Do remember, though, that once seated at such a temporary surface, people will still require just as much space as they would at a permanent bar or table. The difference is that such space can be put to other uses at other times, so providing a flexibility you may find invaluable.

A relaxing and play area

Another aspect of the kitchen as a family room is that the family will often wish to share the room with those who are cooking without participating themselves. The eating zone will be used regularly by such visitors outside mealtimes, but when young children are involved, the situation needs a little thought and planning. It used to be thought that young children and cooking can never mix safely and this is true in the sense that, unless conscious provision is made for them, children can certainly be a hazard in the kitchen. However, experience shows that at most times young children wish to be in visual and verbal contact with the person or people working there, but are quite happy to have their own territory within which they will continue to play so long as they are kept busy.

A play area can often be created by adapting an eating area, so long as some nearby space exists for storing toys. It can be as simple as ensuring that a peninsula is wide enough to enable you to work on one side and the children to play on the other without clashing. In practice this means a surface at least 3 ft (900 mm) and preferably 4 ft (1200 mm) wide. Try to arrange matters so that access to the rest of the house, the garden and especially the lavatory does not mean passing through the main kitchen working areas.

PUTTING IT ALL TOGETHER

The best way to plan the layout of a small kitchen is first to work out where your key work zones should be and what equipment and other items will be stored in each. Only then should you begin to consider what cupboards, shelves and other sorts of storage furniture you require. Most people tackle the job the other way round, by measuring the room and working out what cupboards can be fitted into the space available and then worrying about where everything should be stored in them. This approach tends to lead to unbalanced designs and wasteful use of space.

Start off by creating scale drawings of the floor space and of each of the walls in the room (which designers call elevations). The most convenient scale, which is now used by most designers, is the metric 1 in 20 system whereby every centimetre or inch on your paper represents 20 centimetres or inches in the room. Buy a scale rule with a 1:20 ratio on it from a stationer to help you.

Once you have these drawings, which do not need to be super-accurate at this stage, pencil in approximately where you wish to place each of the main work zones. Start with the sink and dishwashing zone, then place the mixing zone and oven on one side and the cooking zone on the other. There is no fixed rule about which side of the sink each of these should be, so simply do what feels right to you. However, it is a good idea, if you can, to place the serving and eating areas (if you have them as separate zones) between the cooking zone and the way through to the rest of the house.

Having done this, work out how much worktop space you require (or can fit) in each of the zones and then sketch in on the floor plan and elevations where the equipment will be placed. Movable items, such as plug-in electrical appliances, may need to be shown twice, both where they are used and where they should be stored.

Next you should note in pencil on the elevations the positions in which the food, utensils, crockery and other contents ought to be stored. Only when you have done this, should you start sketching in the furniture, selecting closed cupboards, open shelves, pull-out drawers or baskets or other alternatives according to what is to be stored in them and the degree of accessibility you require.

Working out all these things on the elevations means that the correct decisions will be made right at the outset about where items you use often are to be kept, and also that built-in equipment is

placed at the correct height to suit the users. You will then be able to determine whether the particular furniture range that you are considering contains the storage elements you require.

Because the range of options offered by different furniture-makers varies considerably, you may well be frustrated to discover that, if you order furniture from a company whose styles you like, they do not provide items that are necessary to fit your plan. This becomes a real difficulty if, for example, they cannot offer a housing for the type of built-in equipment you have in mind or the housings they do offer set the oven or fridge at the wrong height.

It is not unusual to come across kitchens in which built-in ovens in particular are set too high or too low for the person using them. If you have chosen an oven with an eye-level grill, this should be built in so that the grill pan in the top position is just a few inches below your eye height, so that you do not have either to bend or stretch to see how things are cooking. What often happens is that the furniture-maker adapts a housing which has been designed for a different oven completely and as a result much of the potential convenience, safety and comfort of the eye-level grill is wasted.

Most good quality fitted kitchen furniture provides for worktops being set at a height to suit the purchaser, yet very few people take advantage of this option. To work out the correct worktop height, measure the height, from the floor, of the elbow joint of the person who uses the kitchen most and take away 6 in. (150 mm). This will give you the height of the worktop into which your sink should be set and if the sink itself is not more than 6½ in. (160 mm) deep, you will be able to wash up in it without bending and avoid one of the main causes of backache.

The worktop will be too high for chopping or hand-mixing in comfort. For these purposes, and ideally for hob cooking too, a second surface 4 in. (100 mm) lower should be provided, which may be at an angle to the main worktop or take the form of a centre table or peninsula. Note that in most cases this will be slightly higher than normal dining table height, but will still be practical for kitchen eating. If the kitchen is used regularly by a number of people who differ widely in elbow height, the compromise worktop height should tend to favour those who are shorter. However, in such cases the need for two levels of worktop in the kitchen will be even greater.

There is no merit in making the sizes of the

main work zones any greater than those indicated on the preceding pages. If you decide to provide extra space outside the central working area for special purposes, that is another matter, but simply making a kitchen bigger does not make it better to work in. One of the reasons why people often feel their kitchens are too small when, if properly planned, they are not, is that they have fallen into the trap of fitting lots of simple base and wall cupboards and yards of working surfaces. The resulting waste of storage space gives the impression that you need more, when in reality you need to make proper use of the potential for storage between hip and shoulder height.

CRITICAL DIMENSIONS

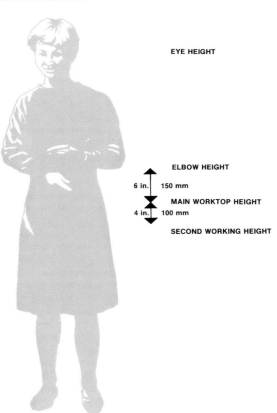

EYE HEIGHT

ELBOW HEIGHT

6 in. | 150 mm

MAIN WORKTOP HEIGHT

4 in. | 100 mm

SECOND WORKING HEIGHT

A person who for some years has had a kitchen with yards of working surfaces probably cannot imagine that a working area involving less apparent worktop space could possibly be adequate. However, if you do not have to use much of your worktop area for ready-to-hand storage during food preparation and cooking and most of the items you need can be reached without stretching where they are normally stored, you will actually need less worktop space. As a result your main working area can be more compact and will be far less tiring to work in.

The spacing that you plan between separate furniture elements is also important. If your kitchen contains two parallel worktops or a worktop and a peninsula which are both part of the main working area, in most cases these should not be less than 40 in. (1000 mm) or more than 60 in. (1500 mm) apart. The minimum space allowance may be reduced to as little as 36 in. (900 mm) if there is only one main user of the kitchen and so long as the space is not a throughway to a door. If it is, the minimum space should be increased to 48 in. (1200 mm) and the maximum could be increased to 72 in. (1800 mm).

If two items of furniture are set either side of a corner in which there is a door out of the room or to a separate larder or store room, ideally the space to pass between them should not be less than 34 in. (850 mm) and never less than 30 in. (750 mm).

Finally, in planning your new kitchen layout ensure that you make full use of space in corners. They are ideal for siting a big larder or store cupboard, or the sink or cooking hob, which will leave space free along an adjoining wall for a food mixing or serving area that might not otherwise have been feasible.

In carrying out such a kitchen planning exercise you will discover numerous problems of awkward sizes, clashes over the use of space and difficulties in fitting the storage you require into each area. It is at this stage that the help of an experienced kitchen designer will be of real value and you will be able to understand his or her advice far better for having attempted the exercise yourself.

Most designers will agree that the best kitchens are created jointly by an experienced planner and customers who really understand what they want to achieve in practical and visual terms. Once you have listed your needs and worked out some sort of layout scheme, you will at least be able to offer the designer a detailed brief and measure whether or not the proposals put forward really meet your requirements.

IDEAL SPACINGS

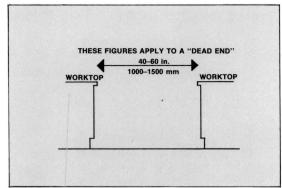

THESE FIGURES APPLY TO A "DEAD END"
40–60 in.
1000–1500 mm
WORKTOP   WORKTOP

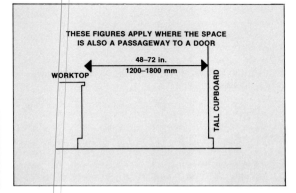

THESE FIGURES APPLY WHERE THE SPACE IS ALSO A PASSAGEWAY TO A DOOR
48–72 in.
1200–1800 mm
WORKTOP   TALL CUPBOARD

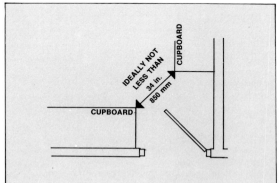

CUPBOARD
IDEALLY NOT LESS THAN 34 in. 850 mm
CUPBOARD

SUPPLIERS

Suppliers' names and principal addresses are printed in bold. UK agents and/or addresses, where these differ from the main entry, are in light type.

AEG
AEG Nuremberg, PO Box 1036, Muggenhoferstrasse 135, D-8500 Nuremberg, Germany
AEG, 217 Bath Road, Slough, Berkshire SL1 4AW

Allmilmö
Milewski Mobelwerk Zeil KG, D-8729 Zeil am Main, Postfach 1180, Germany
48 The Broadway, Thatcham, Nr Newbury, Berkshire RG13 4HP

Alno
Alno-Mobelwerke GmbH & Co KG, Postfach 1160, D-7798 Pfullendorf, Germany
Unit 10, Hampton Farm Industrial Estate, Hampton Road West, Hanworth, Middlesex TW3 6DB

Arc Linea
Arc Linea Arredamentispa, V. Le Pasubio 50, 36030 Caldogno, Vicenza, Italy
32 Store Street, London WC1E 7BS

Ariston
Merloni Elettrodomestici Spa, Viale A. Merloni 45, 60044 Fabriano, Italy
Ariston Domestic Appliances Ltd, Merloni House, 20 Kennett Road, Crayford, Kent DA1 4QN

ATAG
ATAG Keukentechniek B.V., Postbus 8, 7070 AA Ulst, Netherlands
19-20 Hither Green, Clevedon, Avon BS21 6XU

Robert Bosch
Hansfeierabend GmbH, Postfach 286, 3352 Einbeck 1, Germany
The Quadrangle, Westmount Centre, Uxbridge Road, Hayes, Middlesex UB4 0HD

R.E.A. Bott
Crown House, Uxbridge Road, Rickmansworth, Hertfordshire WD3 2AZ

Bulthaup
Bulthaup GmbH & Co, D-8318 Aich Uber Landshut, Germany
37 Wigmore Street, London W1

Canon (UK) Ltd
Gough Road, Bilston, West Midlands WV14 8XR

Corian
DuPont Co, Wilmington, Delaware 19898, USA
C.D. UK Ltd, Unit 8, Centre 27, Bankwood Way, Birstall, West Yorkshire WS17 9TB

Czecn & Speake Ltd
39c Jermyn Street, London SW1Y 6DN

Elon
Elon Tiles (UK) Ltd, 8 Clarendon Cross, Holland Park, London W11 4AP

Franke
Ch-4663 Aarburg, Switzerland
East Park, Manchester International Office Centre, Styal Road, Manchester M22 5WB

Gaggenau
Gaggenau Werke, Eisenwerkstrasse, D-7560 Gaggenau, Baden, Germany
Gaggenau Electric (UK) Ltd, Gaggenau House, Unit 2, Heathrow Summit Centre, West Drayton, Middlesex

Halotrak
Bearwarden House, Royston Road, Wendends Ambo, Saffron Walden, Essex CB1 4JX

CP Hart
CP Hart & Sons Ltd, Newnham Terrace, Hercules Road, London SE1 7DR

Hathaway Country Kitchens
Clifford Mill, Clifford Chambers, Nr Stratford-upon-Avon, Warwickshire CV37 8HW

Insinkerator
4700 21st Street, Racine, Wisconsin 53406, USA
Chelmsford Road, Great Dunmow, Essex CM6 1LP

Jenn-Air
Jenn-Air Corp, 3035 Shadeland, Indianapolis, Indiana 46226-1901, USA

Kenwood
Kenwood Ltd, New Lane, Havant, Hampshire PO9 2NH

Kohler
The Kohler Co, Kohler, Wisconsin 53044, USA

Kontinental Housecraft
Bearwarden House, Royston Road, Wendens Ambo, Saffron Walden, Essex CB1 4JX

Leicht
Leicht Einbaukuchen GmbH, D-7070 Schwabisch Bmund, Germany
Leicht Furniture Ltd, Leicht House, Lagoon Road, Orpington, Kent BR5 3QG

Miele & Cie
Carlmiele 29, Gutersloh, Germany
Fairacres, Marcham Road, Abingdon, Oxfordshire OX14 1TW

Neff
Neff Munich, Hochstrasse 11, 8000 Munich 80, Germany
Neff (UK) Ltd, The Quadrangle, Westmount Centre, Uxbridge Road, Hayes, Middlesex UB4 0HD

Nutone
Madison and Red Bank Roads, Cincinnati, Ohio 45227, USA
32 Harmer Street, Gravesend, Kent DA12 2AX

Poggenpohl
Poggenpohl GmbH, Herringhausterstrasse 33, Postfach 2455, D-4900 Herford, Germany
2nd floor, Silbury Court, 368 Silbury Boulevard, Milton Keynes MK9 2AF

Sanyo
Sanyo Electric Co Ltd, Osaka, Japan
Sanyo House, Otterspool Way, Watford, Hertfordshire

SAV UK Ltd
Scandia House, 131 Armfield Close, West Molesey,
Surrey KT8 2JR

Sharp
Sharp Corporation of Japan, 2222 Magaike-Cho,
Abeno-Ku, Osaka 545, Japan
Sharp House, Thorpe Road, Newton Heath, Manchester
M10 9BE

SieMatic
SieMatic Mobelwerke GmbH, August-Siekmanstrasse
1-5, D-4972 Loehne 1, Germany
SieMatic (UK) Ltd, 11-17 Fowler Road, Hainault Industrial
Estate, Ilford, Essex IG6 3UU

Smallbone & Co (Devizes) Ltd
Hopton Industrial Estate, London Road, Devizes,
Wiltshire SN10 2EU

Siemens
Siemens-Electrogerate GmbH, Hochstrasse 17,
D-8000 Munich 80, Germany
The Quadrangle, Westmount Centre, Uxbridge Road,
Hayes, Middlesex UB4 0HD

Tefal (UK) Ltd
11-49 Station Road, Langley, Slough, Berkshire
SL3 8DR

Tielsa
Tielsa Kuchen GmbH, Industriestrasse 14-18, D-4902
Bad Salzuflen 1, Germany
Wakefield Road, Gildersome, Leeds LS2 0QW

Tricity
Limberline Road, Hilsea, Portsmouth, Hampshire
HP3 5JJ

Villeroy & Boch
Villeroy & Boch AG, Keramische Werke KG, D-6642
Mettlach 1, Germany

Vola
I P Lund Trading APS, Axel Kiers Vej 12, Dk-8270
Hojbjerg, Denmark
Vola UK, Venus Bath Centre, Unit 12, Ampthill Business
Park, Station Road, Ampthill, Bedfordshire MK45 2QW

White-Westinghouse International Corporation
10 Parkway Center, Pittsburgh, Pennsylvanie 15220,
USA

Wicanders (GB) Ltd
Stoner House, Kilnmead, Crawley, West Sussex
RH10 2BG

Woodgoods
Unit 40, Woolmer Trading Estate, Bordon, Hampshire
GU35 9QZ

Woodstock
23 Pakenham Street, London WC1X 0LB

INDEX

Figures in bold relate to illustrations

INDEX

ACKNOWLEDGEMENTS

The publishers gratefully acknowledge the assistance provided by the following in the preparation of this book:
AEG, Jenn-Air (R.E.A. Bott), Imperial (R.E.A. Bott), Gaggenau and Nutone.

PICTURE CREDITS

8–9 Allmilmö, 10 David Mavott, 11 Arclinea, 12–13 Anthony Curtiss, 14–15 Images, 16–17 Schiffini, 19 David Ashby, 20 Gaggenau/Images, 21 **T** Gaggenau/Images, **B** Atag, 22–23 Anthony Curtiss, 24 Anthony Curtiss, 25 **L** Tricity, **R** Domix, 26 Tefal, 27 Black and Decker, 28 AEG/Images, 29 **L** Gaggenau, **R** Jenn-Air/Images, 30 Gaggenau/Images, 31 **L** TI New World, **R** Imperial/Images, 32 Neff, 33 **L** AEG/Images, **R** Westinghouse, 34 **L** Anthony Curtiss, **R** Imperial/Images, 35 AEG/Images, 36 Anthony Curtiss, 37 Nutone/Images, 38 Bosch, 39 **L** Bosch, 40 Peter Aaron/Esto, 41 Poggenpohl, 43 **L** SIC, **R** Annet Held, 44 Bulthaup, 45 David Ashby, 46 David Ashby, 47 **L** David Ashby, **R** Thorn EMI, 48 G. Chabaneix/Slide Press, 49 Peo Eriksson/IMS/Camera Press, 50 Bulthaup, 51 Jahreszeiten Verlag, 52 David Ashby, 53 Bulthaup, 54 Miele, 55 **L** Xey, **R** SeiMatic, 56 Bosch, 57 Bulthaup, 58 **T** SieMatic, **B** Bulthaup, 59 **L** Bulthaup, **R** Marcus Harrison, 60 Poggenpohl, 61 **L** Poggenpohl, **R** Tielsa, 62 Xey, 63 Villeroy and Boch, 65 Bosch, 66 Xey, 67 Bosch, 68 Emmett Bright, 69 Bulthaup, 71 **TL** and **R** Annet Held, **B** Corian, 72 **L** Annet Held, **R** Tom Leighton/The National Magazine Co. Ltd., 73 **L** Peo Eriksson/IMS/Camera Press, **R** Neil Lorimer/Elizabeth Whiting and Associates, 74 **TL** Powell Tuck and Partners, **TR** Michael Nicholson/EWA, **BL** Jessica Strang, **BR** Deidi von Schaewen, 75 **TL** Elon Tiles, **TR** Angela Coombes, **BL** SieMatic, **BR** EWA, 76 **CL** Esto, **C** Annet Held, **R** Richard Bryant/Arcaid, 77 **TL** Michael Dunne/EWA, **BL** Jessica Strang, **C** Hathaway, **TR** Spike Powell/EWA, 78–9 Richard Bryant/Arcaid, 80 Tim Street-Porter/EWA, 81 Spike Powell/EWA, 82 **L** Arclinea, **R** SIC, 83 SIC, 84–5 Annet Held, 86 Ron Sutherland, 87 EWA, 88 Belle/Camera Press, 89 Bulthaup, 90 Richard Bryant/Arcaid, 91 Tim Street-Porter/EWA, 92 **TL** Annet Held, **BL** SIC, **R** Michael Nicholson/EWA, 93 H. Brejat/Slide Press, 94–95 Jerry Tubby/EWA, 96 Annet Held, 97 **L** SIC, **R** Belle/Camera Press, 98 Michael Dunne/EWA, 99 Michael Dunne/EWA, 100 Richard Bryant/Arcaid, 101 Michael Nicholson/EWA, 102–103 Deidi von Schaewen, 104–105 Annet Held, 106–107 SIC, 108–113 Deidi von Schaewen, 114–117 Woodstock, 118–121 Femina/Camera Press, 122–123 Images, 124–125 Kim Sayer, 126–127 Woodgoods, 128–129 Roma Jay, 130–131 MB/Images, 132–133 Neil Lorimer/EWA, 134–135 Michael Nicholson/EWA, 136 Jessica Strang, 137 Jahreszeiten Verlag, 139 **T** Leicht, **B** Anthony Curtiss, 140 Bulthaup, 142 Jahreszeiten Verlag, 143 Woodstock, 144 David Brittain/The National Magazine Co. Ltd., 145 Richard Bryant/Arcaid, 146–147 Living Magazine, 148 Bulthaup, 149 Gaggenau, 150 Finch/Design Council, 152–153 Anthony Curtiss, 154–161 David Ashby.